Teaching That Bears Fruit

"*...still the best Sunday School book available.*"
Dr. Ken Hemphill, Special Assistant to the President for denominational relations at North Greenville University.

"This is a great resource. Everyone should have a copy!"
Tim Smith, Sunday School Open Groups Ministry Leader, Georgia Baptist Convention

"*Thank you for writing this incredible resource to facilitate the Great Commission. Your book is the most concise and teachable "Teacher Education" book that I have seen.*" Dr. Jimmy Wilson, Minister of Adult Education, First Baptist Church Loganville, GA and Professor, Luther Rice Seminary

"*I was one of those "Dump Truck Teachers" (chapter one). I would study all week and then on Sunday morning I would try to dump everything I had studied on my learners. It wasn't working. Thanks to George and "Teaching That Bears Fruit," we now share information that "we" have learned, both from study and experience. And it does make a difference!*" Clarence Cooley, Sunday School Teacher, Acworth, GA

TEACHING THAT BEARS FRUIT

George L. Yates

Springfield, Kentucky

TEACHING THAT BEARS FRUIT
Copyright © 2001, George L. Yates
Reprint 2006
All Rights Reserved. No part of this publication may be reproduced,
stored in a retrieval system or transmitted in any form or by any means
– electronic, mechanical, photocopy, recording or any other – except
for brief quotations in printed reviews, without the
prior permission of the author.
All Scriptures quotations, unless otherwise marked, are from *The Holy
Bible, New International Version*. Copyright © 1973, 1978, 1984 International Bible Society. Used by permission of Zondervan Publishing House. All rights reserved. Scriptures marked KJV from *The Holy
Bible, King James Version*. Copyright © 1977, 1984, Thomas Nelson
Inc., Publishers.

AUTHOR: Yates, George L.,
TITLE: Teaching That Bears Fruit
PUBLISHER: *Sonlight Publishing*
ISBN: 978-0-9988852-3-0
SUBJECT: Christian education

**For more information or
to order additional copies, please contact:**
George Yates
Son C.A.R.E. Ministries
http://soncare.net

Contents

Acknowledgments 7
Introduction 9

Chapter 1 13
Are We Teaching? Are They Learning?
- To Teach
- To Learn
- Rote Memorization vs. Understanding

Chapter 2 31
Teaching Methods, Learning Styles
- Origins of Today's Christian Education Setting
- Natural Learning Abilities
- Learning Styles
- Teaching Methods

Chapter 3 45
Jesus' Approach To Learning
- Discovery Learning
- Object Lessons
- Illustrations, Stories, and Parables
- Teachable Moments
- Practice

Chapter 4 71
The Art of The Question
- Using Questions to Gather Information
- A Quest For Prior Learning
- Making Statements Through Questions
- Open-Ended Questions
- Become a Student of the Question

Chapter 5 85
Curriculum and Application Driven Teaching
    Curriculum
    Application

Chapter 6 101
Evidences of Learning
    Qualifiers of Spiritual Maturity

Chapter 7 115
Preparation
    Jesus' Preparation
    Resources for Preparation
    Routine for Preparation
    Time for Preparation
    Prayerful Preparation
    IFPAC

Chapter 8 131
Interactive Learning
    Incorporating Jesus' Approaches to Interactive Learning
    Debriefing
    Moving Beyond Lecture to Interactive

Chapter 9 141
Time Thieves of Christian Education
    Exposing Time Thieves
    Curriculum Time Thieves—Busyness
    Hidden Agenda
    Classroom Oriented Time Thieves
    Fellowship Time, Prayer Request, Teacher Overkill

Conclusion 153
Endnotes 157

Acknowledgments

A sincere and heartfelt thank you to all those who helped make this book a reality.

To Jerry Atkins, my friend, my Pastor, for your support, prayers, and love. You are a friend and a brother, indeed.

To Barry Dollar, my friend and partner in ministry for your valuable input and the impressive cover design.

To Wendy Hollingsworth, for your editing expertise. Thanks for your hours of work and editorial insight.

To the members of First Baptist Church, Kettering, Ohio and Eastwood Baptist Church, Marietta, Georgia. Thank you for allowing me to challenge you and in some cases, for your willingness to venture out into unknown territory. Without your prayers and support this work would never have come to fruition.

To the most significant person in my life, my wife, Pam. You are my support, my encourager, my Proverbs 31 woman. You have given more than anyone to see this work accomplished. I love you dearly and stand exceedingly grateful to have you by my side!

Most of all to my Lord, and Savior. God alone could provide the insight and workmanship to a vessel such as I. Thank you Father. May you use this, your work, to change lives far reaching, for years to come.

Introduction

Several good books have been written in the last few years concerning the teaching methods of our day. Some of these books have inspired the writings compiled to form this book. My challenge in these writings is to stir the thought processes of Christian educators and pastors across the nation and beyond. The intent of this book is to encourage you, the reader, to look at your own teaching educating process, to determine its effectiveness and to stimulate the creative ability inside you. My prayer is that during this process you will allow the Holy Spirit to increase your teaching ability and greatly enhance the education process between you and your learners.

One of the great fallacies of our day is that if we study enough, gather as much information as we can and carry all that we can into the classroom or pulpit, we can teach an effective lesson. The main objection I have with this theory and common practice is that it goes against all human learning processes. I call this common practice the Content-Dump-Truck Method. Many of our classrooms and pulpits today are filled with content-driven leaders. Teachers spend several hours each week pouring over twenty-seven sets of commentaries and the Internet for theological commentary. Then on Sunday morning (or the given day for our class to meet) we enter the classroom with high anticipation of sharing all that we have learned this week in our studies. This is good and commendable for our own self-study. However, to approach a class this way is like backing a dump truck into the class and in twenty-five to thirty minutes dumping on our learners, everything that we have gleaned from several hours of research over a period of several days.

A greater tragedy in this method is that rarely do we give our learners any means of carrying this content into their own lives. In other words there is no application. I can give you all the Bible scripture and commentary that I can possibly find, yet if I do not assist you in how to apply the truths of scripture to your life, I have not taught you one thing, other than facts and figures. One writer has put it this way, "It does not matter how good the medicine is, unless someone swallows it and is healed."

Many times the person not factored into the equation of the learning experience is the learner. Too often, when we do not see expected life-change in our learners or when no one is "stepping up to the plate" to serve, we tend to blame the learner. While some of the responsibility lies with the learner, rarely is the thought entertained that the teacher, educator bear some of the responsibility. This book is devoted

Introduction

to helping Christian educators "improve their serve" and create life-changing learning.

In many education settings we do not give our listeners time or opportunity to exercise the learning process. We can give definitive answers and absolutes. We can teach the Bible as history, information, facts, and figures. But if we want spiritual transformation to take place in the lives of our listeners, we must allow them to become learners. Many believers walk in and out of churches week after week with no real learning because we have not allowed or challenged them to become learners. When we do not allow our listeners to become learners, we are guilty of not allowing them to practice James 1:22; *"Be ye doers of the Word, and not hearers only"* (KJV). We question why there is no "fruit" in their lives and many times we need to look no farther than the mirror.

If we provide the proper equipping we can see changed lives. Evidences of learning can be found in our learners. We must provide the equipping. We must teach for life-change. A seed placed alone on a shelf, or in a barrel with thousands of other seeds will never produce fruit. However, if placed in fertile soil, and cared for in the proper manner, one single seed will produce, *"...thirty, sixty, and a hundred fold."* (Mark 4:8b)

As you read this book, I trust you will take each facet, chapter, principle and truth and examine your own teaching process. Each time you sit down to read a portion of this book, first take a moment to pray, asking the Holy Spirit to guide you and be your teacher through your reading. If you will examine each precept and practice discussed in this book, allowing the Holy Spirit's influence to improve and increase your teaching capacity, you will see improvements. Improvements in your teaching abilities, in class participation, and in the changed lives of those you lead. May God bless you in your efforts and endeavors to continually strengthen your abilities! Teach for life-change! Teach to bear fruit!

Chapter One

Are We Teaching?
Are They Learning?

In the summer of my twentieth year, I worked on the maintenance and grounds crew for a local harness racing track. It was a good experience for several reasons. One being I learned to drive everything from golf carts to farm tractors and 5,000 gallon water trucks to the track dump truck. The water truck and dump truck were my favorites, aside from the track owner's Cadillac. I had to keep the water truck on the premises. However, the dump truck, I was able to drive all over Jefferson County making pick-ups and deliveries.

This truck had ten gears and I used them all. First gear, known as granny, was a very low gear and reached top speed at about two miles an hour. It wasn't much use unless you had a full load and were starting up an incline from a dead stop. If you tried to use it any other time it only caused problems and seemed to place everyone following behind the truck in a very bad mood.

The other thing I remember about that dump truck is that the guys with experience driving it could raise the bed and empty the load in a smooth manner. When I tried, the entire load (normally finely ground limestone) seemed to come out in one huge pile — at least when I first started. The load was not applicable in the configuration of a huge pile as I dumped it. To fulfill its purpose, someone else (an entire crew) had to come in and rake, scoop, and shovel making a smooth and usable surface.

Christian education has in many ways taken on some of the characteristics of the dump truck. Many classrooms and pulpits are filled each week with a teacher/preacher who has spent several hours the previous week gleaning from several commentaries and surfing the web for as much theological material as possible on the scriptures concerning this week's lesson. There is nothing wrong with this in and of itself. In fact these leaders are to be commended for their commitment and effort. However, the downfall comes when they stand behind the pulpit or in front of the class. We have gained so much knowledge and insight to this set of scriptures that we do not want our students to miss out on any part of it. Therefore, we back our truck up in the classroom each week and raise the bed and dump it all on our students. Most of the time it is like my first few tries with the dump truck. It all comes out in one heaping pile. Like the limestone, it is not usable in one huge pile.

Information, facts, and knowledge do not create learning. They do create an unpleasant and unsightly mound that is not applicable in the lives of our learners. Most of us do not have the luxury of having a clean-up crew coming in behind us to work the mound into a usable surface of transforming wisdom.

The other thing I see happening is teachers and preachers trying to drive their class in that low granny gear. As this transpires our listeners become like those following the slow moving truck. Our learners are bored and want to know, "When are you going to shift gears and drive this thing."

FREEZE-FRAME
With these two scenarios in place—driving in low gear, and dumping our load in an unusable manner—what are we doing to our learners? What exactly are we teaching them? Are they learning what we think we are teaching?

TO TEACH

To answer these questions lets take a look at the terms teaching and learning. What does the dictionary say concerning these two terms?

> **Teach:** to impart knowledge or skill; to cause to learn by example or experience; Synonyms of teach: instruct, train, and tutor.[1]

For further examination, let's take a look at the Greek word for 'teach' used in the New Testament. The most commonly used word is "*didasko.*" The definition of *didasko* is *the act of causing someone to learn.* If I had two tennis balls in my hand, which of the following would best represent the definition of *didasko*? First, I come to you and ask you to hold out your hand. Informing you that I want to give you one of the tennis balls, I release the ball to gently roll down my hand, off my fingers and into your hand. After this I turn to your neighbor and say, "Catch this ball." However, before he can react I throw the second ball in the opposite direction, out of his reach. Which best illustrates *didasko*?

The depiction using the first ball does, doesn't it? The difference is, I prepared you in how to receive the ball — I asked you to hold out your hand. Second, I gave the reason I wanted you to hold out your hand. Then, I allowed the ball to gently roll off my hand and into yours. My actions caused you to receive the ball. It was a gentle, informative act causing you to receive the ball. Didasko — teaching is the act of causing someone to learn. The actions with the second ball may have taught something but it certainly was not didasko. Yet, I am convinced the action with the second ball represents many of the classrooms and pulpits across our nation today. We have all sorts of gathered information and we hurriedly throw it out in the classroom, usually not even in reach of our learners.

The writers of the four gospels use the word

Are We Teaching? Are They Learning?

didasko to describe Jesus' teaching. Of the eighty-four times the word teach or one of its derivatives appears in the New Testament, fifty-eight are translated from didasko. Two of these references are found in Matthew 5:19 and Mark 6:34.

> *"...whoever shall do and teach them, the same shall be called great in heaven."* Matthew 5:19

> *"And Jesus, when He came out, saw much people, and was moved with compassion toward them, because they were as sheep not having a shepherd: and he began to teach them many things."* Mark 6:34

In Matthew 5:19 Jesus is giving us a directive, telling us to '*didasko*' — guide others in the learning process. The emphasis here is on the learner. Mark 6:34 is an illustration of Jesus teaching. In this verse not only does the word teach (*didasko*) place the emphasis on the learner, the author tells us Jesus "*was moved with compassion toward them*" and even gives a description of the compassion, "*as sheep without a shepherd.*" The entire verse demonstrates how Jesus places the emphasis on His learners. As you study Jesus' teachings you will find He always places the emphasis on His learners. It is never on the teacher. He is always in the act of effecting changed lives.

The art of *didasko* has been lost somewhere in the last 2,000 years. The intent of writing this book is to help Christian educators return to *didasko* — teaching the way Jesus taught. In all of Jesus' teachings He never used mass amounts of information, facts, and knowledge. His teaching approaches caused His listeners to become learners. Jesus' teaching ministry, His life, was about changing lives. Jesus' every move was an act of "causing others to learn."

Producing An Effect

Both Webster's description of teach and the Greek definition of *didasko* use the word *cause* in the definition. How do we cause someone to learn? Let's look up the word cause.

Cause: Something that produces an effect, result, or consequence.[2]

According to this definition, what we as teachers bring to the classroom should produce some type of result. It should have a changing effect on people's lives. One recurring theme you will read in this book is that true learning brings about a personal change in behavioral lifestyle. That is why I believe the word cause is found in the description of both teach and didasko. Our aim is to teach for life-change, the act of causing life-change. That is transformational teaching and it is the way Jesus taught.

Freeze Frame

Is your teaching producing life change in your learners? What evidences can be found in your student's lives, which can be attributed to the Holy Spirit's use of your teaching this last month? In the last six months? How about the past year?

Are We Teaching? Are They Learning?

Perhaps after contemplating the questions in the last freeze frame you could not think of any true-life behavioral change among your listeners in recent times. If so, I would tell you two things. First, you are not alone. If the truth were known I believe statistics would more than likely show at least ninety-five percent of all Christian educators would have come to the same conclusion. Second, do not get discouraged, it is not time to throw in the towel. Hang on to your bootstraps because you are about to take a journey that will change your preparation and teaching habits for life. Stop right now and pray asking God to use this book under the Holy Spirit's guidance to bring about a life-change in you. A change that will not only revolutionize your teaching, but will impact lives for all time and eternity.

TO LEARN

We have looked at teaching. Now let us turn our attention to a few thoughts on learning.

> **FREEZE FRAME**
>
> *What is true learning? How do we gauge learning? Are the standards we use in Christian education to determine learning adequate?*

Learn: To gain knowledge, comprehension, or mastery of; to acquire through experience.[3]

If the definition of learning is to gain knowledge,

comprehension, or mastery of something or to acquire through experience, how do we apply that to Christian education? Earlier in this chapter, I made the statement that true learning brings about behavioral life-change. Allow me a few moments to dissect Webster's definition using this statement.

Perhaps you have heard the story of the house of John 3:16. The story tells of a young boy, homeless and all alone on the city streets on a cold, wet, and rainy night. A policeman finds the boy and tells him to go to a certain house and when the lady answers the door tell her, "John 3:16 sent me." The boy does as the policeman suggested and the woman of the house invites him in. First, she gets him out of his wet clothes, gives him a warm bath, fresh clothes, a hot meal, and a fire to warm himself by, not to mention a soft feather bed to sleep in for the night. As each event unfolds during the evening the boy keeps repeating this statement, "I don't know what this John 3:16 is, but it sure makes a young boy feel good." The woman of the house shares the scripture, John 3:16, with the boy and explains that everything she did for him that evening was her way of expressing John 3:16.

WISDOM AND KNOWLEDGE

If learning is to gain knowledge, will knowledge bring about life-change? Not necessarily. You can learn to quote John 3:16 and yet not understand love at all. You can learn facts, figures, statistics and dates by the wagonload. The truth is facts, figures, numbers and dates will not bring about change in your life. However, understanding them and placing them in proper perspective within the confines of your life and your environmental culture, can definitely bring about change. Learning facts and figures is gaining knowledge. Knowledge however, does not bring about change. It is when you learn to apply those facts and figures with other acquired knowledge that brings about change. God has given us a word for this formula. It is *wisdom.* Wisdom brings about change, knowledge does not. "Wisdom" is life-change.

The second part of Webster's definition says to learn brings about comprehension. Comprehension depicts more than simply understanding. It is mentally grasping onto the subject matter and being able to apply that matter or the truth behind it to life's situations. Comprehension is more than an insight and awareness. It goes beyond those to an intellectual perception with the ability to administer the precepts of the subject being covered. Application and administer are action words. "Action" is life-change.

MASTERING THROUGH APPLICATION

The third term in Webster's definition of learn is "to master" or "the mastery of." To have mastery of a subject is to have full command of the subject. It is to have a consummate skill or knowledge of something. In the Asian arts of self-defense, such as karate, the lead teacher has earned the title "Master." This title signifies he knows more of and about the skills of the art being practiced than anyone in his dojo (school). One who has mastery over something is considered an artist of great and exemplary skill. Notice the word skill keeps appearing in the exegesis of this definition. Skill is an applied ability. The only way to know if you have a skill is to apply it or use it. Application not only brings about behavioral or life-change. "Application" is life-change.

Think about that statement. If someone is applying a truth or principle they have learned they are changing the way they do or perceive something. The very first time you sat in the driver's seat of a car and drove away you actually were applying what you had learned about driving. You were no longer forced to be a passenger. You had taken the necessary steps to bring about change. Someone had to show you how to drive. Your first time out may not have been the most graceful, yet you were willing to apply what you had learned. From that point, you practiced those skills increasing your ability and improving those learned skills.

Though we have a supernatural edge, Christian education must follow the same natural laws of learning. We must not only give our learners facts, information and material, we must equip them with *wisdom* to transform and mature them. You do not learn to drive a car by listening to a lecture on facts, figures and the history of cars. Facts, figures, and history do not teach you *how to* drive.

The *how to* presents the skills you need to drive. In the *how to* process you acquire the wisdom for

Are We Teaching? Are They Learning?

transformation from passenger to driver. Second, there must be some physical *action* that allows you to interact with the car (practice) and demonstrate your newly acquired knowledge (wisdom, skills). That is *application*.

In too many churches we teach the facts, figures, and history in the scriptures, and never move to the more important *how to*. Remember, *didasko* or teaching is the act of causing someone to master something. If we fail to give learners the application — the how to — what are we causing them to master? Are we creating masters of trivia? Or perhaps masters of boredom? Unfortunately, in many of our churches today, people walk out week after week without any true learning. There is no life-change.

LEARNING THROUGH EXPERIENCE

Learn: To gain knowledge, comprehension, or mastery of; to acquire through experience.

The last part of the definition we have been looking at is to acquire through experience. Acquiring is the action of taking something on that is new and different making it part of our being. To acquire is to assimilate something into our very being. We absorb it into our being. It becomes part of us. '*Through experience*' can only be one thing, action. Our actions are the means through which we display our behavior. A changed life is visible through the actions of the learner. Behavioral change is life-change.

With all of this in mind, we can draw the conclusion that true learning occurs when an alteration of the lifestyle or behavior patterns of our learner is evidenced in accordance with our teaching. There is one other factor. You and I are not the teacher. We are only the instruments used by the one and only teacher in Christian education, the Holy Spirit. True learning causes life-change. Teach for life-change!

Kevin, a young man who was recruited to teach in the youth department. Kevin was not given any formal training. Basically, he was handed a set of curriculum materials and told, "Go get 'em." After a couple of years in the youth department, Kevin was frustrated and left his teaching position. A couple of months later, I asked Kevin to sit in on our adult class teachers' meetings. He began attending the meetings and after a few weeks I needed someone to teach one of our young adult classes one Sunday. I asked Kevin if he would fill in for me. A month later, I asked Kevin to fill in again for the same class, which was without a teacher. Kevin came to me and asked about teaching the class until I could find a permanent teacher. Kevin ended up taking the class and for the last three years it has been one of the best growing classes in the church. The class has birthed at least two other classes and produced numerous teachers and Sunday School workers.

Kevin is not from Missouri but he is a "show me" kind of guy. Kevin was not easily convinced by word of mouth. The principles and practices of teaching/learning and class growth had to be proven to him. As the class grew, Kevin would come to me and say, "I learned this from you…" or "You are the one that taught me to…" Kevin has grown eminently in his God-given abilities to teach and lead his class. How has the growth taken place? Was it because he had a good mentor, yours truly? No, not at all!

Kevin attends training and reads books, studies the internet and other material on improving his abilities. He knows the Holy Spirit is his teacher. He has learned to take the knowledge presented him, gain a deserving understanding of it, and then place it in proper perspective. Kevin has utilized God-given wisdom to put into action the application of learned knowledge. Kevin has experienced an alteration of behavior patterns for teaching/leading an adult Sunday School class. He has experienced change and he teaches for life-change.

EMOTION AND LEARNING

One final thought while looking at the teaching and learning aspects of Christian education. We have looked at teaching and at learning and what they are. How do we as Christian educators gauge or evaluate learning? In many cases, it is through scripture memorization — especially with children. While scripture memorization is important and vital to our spiritual walk, it is not an end in itself. We are told to memorize scripture. The Psalmist said, *"Thy word have I hid in my heart, that I might not sin against thee."* Psalm 119:11 (KJV). A person can memorize and quote the entire Bible and not understand what any one verse means. Without application, scripture memorization is rote.

Rote memorization is widely used and accepted in our culture. It is the task of learning something for the purpose of repeating it back. Rote memorization employs short-term memory. True learning employs long-term memory. When information enters our brain it enters our short-term memory bank. Before it can be transferred to our long-term memory it must be attached to an emotion. This is easily realized in life's "hard" lessons. We have encountered scores of wisdom and enlightenment through pain and sorrow. These lessons are easily recalled due to the emotional ties with pain and sorrow we experienced at the time of the learning experience.

This is true of every piece of information you have in your long-term memory even the seemingly simple and mundane things such as telephone numbers. You remember certain phone numbers because you have attached a certain benefit to that set of numbers. You know that by dialing a certain set of numbers in a particular sequence you will be able to talk to someone you know or someone who will benefit you in some other way, i.e. police, pharmacist, grocer, etc. These are attached to our long-term memory by a means other than rote. If rote memorization locked information into our long-term memory, there would be no need in cramming for tests. Rote memorization is not a gauge for learning.

I remember as a child hearing how my Uncle

Are We Teaching? Are They Learning?

Willie was known as the best mechanic in Logan County, Kentucky. Whenever I went to visit my mother's family, I was always in awe at how people would come around and ask for help with their automobiles. It seemed everywhere we went while visiting, someone would bring up Uncle Willie's name and his talent. However, I was never more awestruck and amazed at his talents than when I was eighteen.

I drove my 1965 Mustang to visit Uncle Willie and Aunt Rena. While visiting, Uncle Willie offered to rebuild my carburetor. I took him up on the offer and we went to town to purchase a rebuild kit. Before I continue, you need to understand I have been accused of being a detail-oriented analyst and a perfectionist. Both of those quality characteristics build upon organization and designation. Being mechanically inclined has never appeared in my resume.' After my uncle removed the carburetor from the engine, we sat down across from each other at the picnic table. All he had was a couple of screwdrivers, the carburetor and a small cardboard box. I watched as my uncle began to disassemble the carburetor.

The shocking thing to me was as he began removing screws and springs, tubes, plates and other parts, he threw them all in the small cardboard box. He threw them all in together, without looking. He didn't even pay attention to keep them separated. He just threw them in like they were trash. I almost began to cry. I wanted to yell out, "What are you doing? That's a Holley four barrel high performance carburetor!" When he dumped that small box of mixed parts into an old coffee can half-full of gasoline, I was certain there was no way my car would ever run again until I bought a new carburetor. There was no way even my Uncle Willie was going to be able to put my Holley four-barrel high performance carburetor back together again.

However, when it came time to put it back together, I observed a true master at work. With as much ease as he disassembled the carburetor, every little screw, spring, tube, plate, and part slipped right into place — and not a screw was left over! When he reaffixed it to the car and made a few adjustments, the Mustang fired right up.

My uncle Willie was a master mechanic and he did not learn his trade by memorizing formulas and diagrams in a book. His learning did not come from listening to lectures. His mastery of skills came from experience. He knew how every small piece of that carburetor adjoined and how each piece functioned within the whole unit. I believe he could have rebuilt that carburetor blindfolded. He did not sit down at that picnic table and read the instructions on the rebuild kit before inserting his screwdriver. The knowledge and wisdom he has is locked in his long-term memory. Just as my Uncle Willie is a master mechanic, we need to become master teachers and assist our students in becoming master learners.

Teaching is the transferring of knowledge, information, and material. Teaching does not indicate that learning is taking place. Learning is the acquisition and application of wisdom and information, which brings about transformation and maturity. Notice that teaching does not in any fashion suggest the transferring of wisdom. Wisdom cannot be transferred or taught. Wisdom comes only after the acceptance and application of information to prior learning.

Learning occurs when we attach prior knowledge, wisdom, and experience to the information, knowledge, and material being presented at this current time. The process of connecting the two — prior experience and current information — brings about behavioral life-change. The behavioral or lifestyle change is the evidence of learning. A teacher is a guide. As Christian educators we are leading and guiding our listeners in the learning process.

The dump truck load of information, facts, figures and material does not create life-changing learning. Wisdom, action, and application create life-change. Our calling is to teach for life-change. Jesus invested three years in the lives of His learners. Not only were their lives dramatically changed; empowered by the Holy Spirit they made a major impact on the world, that still exists today. Teach for life-change! This is teaching that bears fruit!

Chapter Two

Teaching Methods, Learning Styles

The computer stopped. It froze up and would not respond to any keystroke or click of the mouse. Being new on the job and not being well-versed in computer technology, the receptionist did not know what to do. Once she realized the computer would not respond, and fearful that she would lose all of the report she had been working on, she asked for help from one of the more experienced secretaries. The secretary walked over, sat down at the receptionist's desk, made a few quick keystrokes, stood up and said, "There you are," and walked away. The receptionist was relieved and went back to work. Within a couple of hours the same thing happened to the receptionist's computer.

The same scenario played out. The next day came and went and the receptionist's computer locked up again. Once again the experienced secretary came to the rescue of the new employee.

Each time the receptionist was embarrassed and did not like pulling the secretary away from her workload. She tried to watch as the secretary freed the computer. But it was to no avail. The secretary would come in, make a few quick keystrokes and be off again. The secretary was very knowledgeable in the workings of the computer. In her mind, she was doing what needed to be done. She was correcting the problem. Or was she? Was she really correcting the problem or just the symptoms?

Frustration was setting in for both ladies. In the secretary's mind the new receptionist was not learning to avoid making the error that was causing the computer to lock up. The receptionist's frustration was with the system and that the secretary wasn't taking time to teach her how to correct the problem or how to avoid it. Had the secretary taken the time to explain the unlocking procedure and possibly tried to help the receptionist discover what she was doing to cause the computer to lock up, time and frustration could have been saved for both of the ladies.

The teacher (secretary) was very knowledgeable. Yet one thing she was overlooking was the student (receptionist) did not yet know the basics of computer operation. Many times we do the same thing in Christian education. It is easy for those of us who have been around Christianity for a lengthy period of time to forget that many of our listeners may be new Christians or non-Christians. We must continually ask ourselves, "Do they know the essentials yet?" Many of today's Christians and church attendees exhibit biblical illiteracy and a shallow faith because we assume they know, understand, and apply more than they actually do. I attribute much of this to the teaching methods we have used for many years. We can never revisit the basics too often.

Where did the church get its teaching formula? Think of how teaching is done in most Christian education settings. In most cases, one person stands in front of the class or congregation and dispenses information. The information shared was garnered through several hours of research and gathered from different sources and writers. Then we bring it in and unload it all in a matter of minutes. This is the dump truck scenario we looked at in the first chapter. Unfortunately, we forget that you don't just grab a knife and a fork and head for the jungle to eat an elephant. Proper preparation must be made and the elephant must be delivered in small portions. How do you eat an elephant? One bite at a time. The same is true in the teaching/learning environment. Be careful not to assume knowledge and understanding where it may not exist. Frequent the essentials. You will never bring a disservice to anyone by revisiting the basics.

Natural Learning

We teach the way we were taught—one person dispenses the information and everyone attending is expected to retain all that is dispensed. Is this our natural learning process? The best way to determine whether or not this is part of our natural learning temperament is to study a group untainted by a regimented system of teaching. I know of only one true cross section of people that would fit this criteria—preschoolers. How do infants and preschoolers learn? They learn through discovery and imitation, do they not? When an infant first begins to develop his/her motor skills, what do they do? An infant tries to use his hands to find out what is in front of him. He may not be able to get his tiny hand around every object, but he can learn about its texture, density, mobility, and temperature. He is learning through the discovery processes God has given him. As his skills develop he learns to use other senses for learning.

When an infant learns that she can grip things in her hand, where does that hand take everything it can grasp? If she can get her hand on it, it goes to her mouth, doesn't it? Why do babies put everything in their mouth? It is a basic step for learning. One basic step that infants and preschoolers do instinctively, yet, we as adults have long forgotten. When something can be grasped with at least three senses, learning will occur. The smallest of children, when placing something in her mouth is using no less than three senses. The first sense used is *sight*. The child first sees the object. Second, she grasps at and *touches* or feels the object. By placing the object in her mouth a third sense, *taste*, comes into action. In many instances all five senses are utilized. If the

Teaching Methods, Learning Styles

object rattles, scratches, squeaks or makes any other noise, the sense of *hearing* enters the learning procedure. On the way to the mouth the sense of *smell* is exercised as well.

A child learns to walk and speak by imitating those around him. A child born in Korea to Korean parents and adopted as an infant by a family living in southern Georgia will speak English with a South Georgia accent. Their physical appearance may divulge their nation of birth, but their speech never will. The same is true of a child born in New York and raised by a family in Moscow, Russia. They will speak the vernacular of those around them. We are not born with a language and dialect. Those are imitated traits, not inherited. As children grow they continue to learn through discovery and imitation.

It is only when children enter the structured education system that this changes. It has been said that the most formidable years of learning are the first five years of a person's life. Yet, it is at this point that we take children and try to restructure their entire learning network. We place them in a class with other children their age, and place one adult in front of them and attempt to retrain them to learn using a setting and techniques that are foreign to them. We train them to abandon the intuitive learning techniques that have worked so well for them their entire lives. I must take a moment here to say a few school systems are changing to use innovative methods to teach children today. Innovative for school systems and churches in North America, that is.

In churches and Christian education we have copied the secular school system teaching strategy. Research shows this teaching method is a primary learning style for only eighteen to twenty-two percent of the adults in America today. Other studies have shown similar results worldwide. The average retention for spoken communication is less than five percent. The best form of retention is through direct experience. The fact is that learning retention increases in direct proportion with learner involvement. Isn't it ironic that the most used teaching methods in our schools and churches produce the least results? In Christian education settings today, we must remove ourselves from simply telling our listeners what is in the Bible and allow our learners to use their natural God-given abilities to discover God's truths. This will bring about true learning — life-changing learning.

Imagine trying to teach someone to operate a computer using the same methodology we use in church. First, listen to a lecture on computers, try to unscramble the word 'megabyte,' look at the manual, memorize small portions of the manual, then bingo, you are a computer expert. How about teaching someone to drive a car? First, listen to a lecture on the history of cars, connect the dots to form a car, find the hidden car parts in a word search puzzle, open the door, get in and drive off. Sounds a little silly, doesn't it? Yet this is what happens in Christian education settings across North America every week.

Teaching Methods, Learning Styles

What are we telling our listeners? Are they learning what we think we are teaching? What they might be learning is, "If God is as boring as this teacher or preacher, count me out!" Or perhaps we are teaching them, "God is mixed up and scrambled and you have to keep looking to find Him, if you can." Some of the exercises we use might lead some persons to believe they need a special "decoder ring" to understand God. We must strive to use teaching methods conducive to the learning styles of our attendees.

> **FREEZE FRAME**
>
> *List some learning exercises that would direct learning through each of the five senses. I have listed some to help you get started.*
>
> *See—dry erase board, visuals, flip charts*
>
> *Hear—small groups, interactive sharing*
>
> *Touch—object lessons*
>
> *Taste—*
>
> *Smell—*

I trust you were able to list several for each category. We will learn more about methods as we look at Jesus' approach to learning in chapters three and four.

LEARNING STYLES

Much has been written over the years concerning learning styles. Depending on whom you read and study you will find different lists and names for the various learning styles. However, most researchers and writers agree there are four basic learning styles. The names that I refer to come from David A. Kolb as found in his book *Experiential Learning: Experience as the Source of Learning and Development:* 1) Convergent, 2) Divergent, 3) Assimilative, and 4) Accommodative.

Throughout this book I suggest that you prepare with your learners in mind. As you prepare your lesson, mentally assess each of the members of your class to best prepare the teaching material for them and how they will respond. For the sake of a better understanding of learning styles, let's say your class is made up of the cast members of the TV shows Andy Griffith and Gilligan's Island. Let's place them with their learning styles.

Convergent learners are known as "thinkers." They construct upon their skills related to abstract thinking and experimentation. Convergent learners apply the skills and knowledge of prior learning to concepts, experiences and information. Their nature as decision-makers and problem solvers, tends to make them extremely analytical. For many convergent learners, their world is one of facts and figures. Convergent learners do well in a lecture-style teaching environment. Other teaching methods to be used with convergent learners are research projects, handouts, illustrations, graphs, charts and practical activities. Convergent learners are visual learners. The percentage of convergent learners in our society today is very low. One generation where we find convergent learners is the PowerBuilder or G.I. genera-

Teaching Methods, Learning Styles

tion. The generation born in the first twenty-five to thirty years of the twentieth century. This is the generation raised in the Depression era. The Professor from Gilligan's Island and Howard Sprague from Andy Griffith were convergent learners.

Divergent learners are known as the "feelers" of our society. Divergent learners are interested in the feelings of others and themselves in the learning experience. Learning comes out of life's experiences. As you recall, in chapter one we brought to light the fact that for information to be placed in our long-term memory, it must first be attached to an emotion. It is emotion that flips information into our long-term memory. Another word for emotion in our society today is "feelings." Life's experiences are deeply seated in emotion. Divergent learners normally have a great command of the imagination and respond well to others. Teaching methods that work well with divergent learners include group problem solving, brainstorming sessions, interaction with others in the learning setting, role-playing, and music. Divergent learners work well in small groups. Mary Ann, Gilligan, Aunt Bee, and Gomer all had divergent learning styles.

The third learning style is Assimilative. Assimilative learners are known as "pragmatists." Pragmatism is the belief that the meaning of a course of action lies within its observable consequences. To assimilate is to take on as part of yourself, that which is around you. Therefore we can assess that assimilative learners learn by absorbing what goes on around them and by applying prior learning to the cause and effect of the current uncertainty. Assimilators learn by incorporating into their behavior based on "felt need" rather than factual information. Assimilative learners are commonly creative thinkers who gravitate to music and the arts. Assimilators use reasoning skills to pull together new models for others to examine. Teaching methods that work well with Assimilators are problem-solving, brainstorming sessions, testimonies, small groups, interaction, case studies, creative projects, and relational projects — projects which draw a correlation between past learning and the current subject of study. Researchers believe more of today's population prefer this learning style than any other. Our class members with assimilative learning styles are Thurston Howell, III, Ginger, and Andy.

The final learning style is Accommodative. Accommodative learners are the "doers" of our society. Willing to aid and assist in the teaching/learning process, Accommodators are a great asset to the learning environment. They are ready for discussion and participation. Accommodative learners learn by doing and easily adjust to changes in teaching environments and methods. They are adaptive, opportunistic, and usually risk-takers. Accommodative learners are competitive, and assertive. Accommodators are also known to be task-oriented. Teaching methods that work well with accommodative learners are role-playing, music, art, and content assignments; methods, which involve physical application in the learning process. Which of our learners are accommodative? The Skipper and Helen Crump had accommodative characteristics.

> **FREEZE FRAME**
>
> *Where would you place these cast members in the four learning styles?*
>
> Mrs. Howell
>
> Ernest T. Bass
>
> Barney Fife
>
> Opie Taylor
>
> Where did you place yourself?

We each have one primary learning style. All others fall secondary. As you have read through these you may have realized that you have some traits from more than one of these. It is very possible that you have one or more traits from each of the four learning styles described above. A further evaluation will show that one of these four is stronger than the other three for every person. However, don't get discouraged if you do not find that one stands out above the other three as your primary learning style. In that situation consider yourself a broad-based learner.

Teachers of all ages must use methods that incorporate several approaches to learning. It is very advantageous for teachers to learn and develop various teaching methods. Certain methods lend themselves to particular subjects. We naturally gravitate to the teaching method that we are most comfortable using. Do not strap yourself in. Explore and develop other methods, which will benefit your learners. Have at your disposal various methods to serve the different learning styles of your members. As you experiment with and practice different methods, you will become more comfortable with and add new techniques to your reserve.

It is greatly probable that you have all four learning styles in your class. It is important to know how each member of your class learns. Getting to know your members will help. Watch, listen and observe your students in and out of class. See how they respond to different situations and different settings they might be in. Learning about your learners and watching how they react in different learning situations will assist you in determining their learning styles.

Affecting Learning

Prepare your lesson with your learners in mind. If you will mentally prepare your lesson with each class member in mind, you will better be able to communicate the learning material. I began practicing this several years ago. As I prepare my lesson through the week, for Sunday School, for instance, I would mentally picture the class, as it would be on Sunday morning. I mentally go around the room and ask myself questions. How will Tom relate to this statement? Sue has gone through a similar situation recently. How will this illustration affect her? What can I use to compel John and Sam to understand this truth?

While asking yourself these questions about each student, consider how it will affect his or her learning and how it can be used to help them share their experiences, assisting you in the teaching process. Proper preparation can procure interaction while allowing you to remain in control of the class. Using this cognitive development as you prepare for each session of your class will assist you in determining which teaching methods to use and how to relate the material and truths more effectively. It is not important that you attach a learning style to each person but that you adapt to your teaching methods by which your class attendees will learn — methods that will transform lives.

The objective of any educational setting is not to teach but that the learners learn. Christian education must move beyond the telling plane and allow our listeners to become active learners. We want the listeners to learn and we must utilize the different methods available to ensure learning takes place every time we meet. A doctor will prescribe an antibiotic for an illness. If that antibiotic does not bring about restoration of health, he prescribes another one, something different. If the first one did not bring about the desired change, the doctor does not continue to use the same prescription.

We need a teaching prescription to restore the health of the church. A prescription to bring about life-change in our learners. If our teaching does not affect change in our listeners, what are we teaching? In some of our churches the same prescription has been in use for forty or fifty years to no avail. The concept behind a medicine is to bring about change in a person's health. If a medicine does not bring about the desired change a different prescription must be tried. In Christian education, the inspiration behind teaching is to bring about change in the learner's spiritual health. If life-change is not occurring, a different prescription (teaching method) must be tried.

Active learning will only come to pass when learners are allowed to participate in the learning process. Spending time studying learning styles will make you a more effective teacher. Developing and using different teaching methods will make you a more efficient teacher. Introduce different methods in your teaching and you will see your class begin to learn at an increased level, and with greater enthusiasm! Teach for life change. This is teaching that bears fruit.

Chapter Three

Jesus' Approach to Learning

To study effective teaching/learning techniques there are various avenues we could travel. We are fortunate to live in an era with several great educators and master teachers that we can learn from. Available to us also today are the writings of great teachers of generations gone by. Today's technology allows us to dissect and analyze teachers, teaching techniques, learners and learning styles. There is an abundance of research accessible via computers and the Internet, local libraries, research firms, and university studies to assist in our pursuit. All of these combined will lead us to certain conclusions. However, the area of research to best show how people learn and how to teach effectively is not found in any compilation of these. It is found in the teaching/learning techniques and approaches of Jesus Christ.

Jesus was "The Master Teacher." The gospels record many teaching experiences in the three ministry years of Jesus. Not only was His teaching environment widely varied. Jesus used a variety of techniques to assist His listeners in their learning as well. In this and the next chapter we will look at some of Jesus' learning approaches. I refer to them as His approaches to 'learning' because He knew what methods to incorporate in His teaching to most effectively communicate life-style and behavioral change in His listeners. Jesus needed only to spend a few hours with Zachaeus to totally transform his life. It was only a few minutes with the Samaritan woman at the well that brought about life transformation.

Jesus used different approaches and teaching methods depending on His audience and the lesson/truth being taught. Regardless of the approach, Jesus always met His learners at their physical, cognitive, spiritual, and emotional position. His teaching experience always held high relevancy to His listeners. Jesus always taught from His learners' context. Knowing that learning builds upon learning, Jesus always began His teaching with His listeners' inclination in mind.

Matthew gives us record of two men coming to Jesus on separate occasions. In Matthew 8:22 Jesus tells the young man to "*Let the dead bury the dead.*" He knew His learner's seat of passion was "home" with

Jesus' Approach to Learning

his family. In verse 21 of chapter 19 Jesus tells the young ruler to, "*go and sell all that you have*". Here He is dealing with possessions not family, because he read the desires of the young ruler's heart. Jesus taught with relevancy to His listeners. He knew 'where they were coming from.' He taught from their context. Jesus taught to bring about life-change.

As we have discussed in earlier chapters, as teachers we must realize that learning our subject matter isn't good enough. We must know how to enable our students to learn the subject matter and live it. What good is all of our knowledge if it does not affect the lives of the people whom God has placed around us? You can have the nicest newest car around, but if you do not have any fuel to drive it, it becomes nothing more than a conversation piece. The same is true with Christian education. You can have all the knowledge — information, facts and figures — available, yet without application it will get you nowhere. It is the application, integration of the principles and truths into our daily routine, which fuels knowledge into life-changing behavior.

I once went on a weekend excursion with three friends. One of these friends was in his late twenties, living at home and generating a good income. He loved to buy things, materialistic things. He had his own boat, a nice car, several firearms, and expensive camera equipment among other things. While on vacation he would pull out his expensive light meter, place certain filters on his camera lens, make adjustments in his aperture and focal settings, double-checking before taking a photograph. I, on the other hand would take my used camera, make estimated adjustments and snap away.

During the entire trip I kept hearing, "Those pictures will never turn out. You need a light meter. You are wasting film." I kept on shooting the way I always had. He kept on tormenting. When we returned home, I had my film processed and gladly showed my work to everyone. I still have those photos some twenty years later. My friend? No one ever saw his photographs. Every time someone would ask about them he would give an excuse. It did not take long to realize that his photos apparently did not come out. Being the nice friends that we were, we did not let him live that one down for a long while.

The point is this, you can have the newest and best equipment money can buy. However, if you do not know how to properly utilize what you have acquired, you'll never create a work of art. I believe God intends for us to use Christian education to become works of art for Him. Not works of art that hang on a wall, or sit in a pew. Rather, laboring works of art. Laboring for His Kingdom. It is not the knowledge, the facts and information that matters. The value is in what each of us does with the knowledge we have. As Christian educators we need to ensure that we are not merely passing along knowledge. We need to be the paintbrush in God's hand, allowing Him to use us to produce great works of art. Our canvas is each learner He has placed in our trust.

Jesus' Approach to Learning

The gospels record many of Jesus' teaching encounters. When we compare Jesus' teaching style to the methods of today we find several interesting distinctions. Jesus very seldom taught in a formal setting. You never see Him in a classroom. In fact most of Jesus' teaching occurred in places that we rarely consider today. Jesus taught on the road while walking with His listeners. He taught on hillsides and at mealtime. He taught in the marketplace and in homes. Jesus taught where life was lived out everyday. Let's spend some time looking at how Jesus taught.

> **FREEZE FRAME**
>
> *Where would we find Jesus teaching if He were here today? Read the last paragraph again and consider where we might find Jesus teaching in the present day. Would most of His teaching take place in a church classroom on Sunday morning? Where and how can we as Christian educator's model Jesus' teaching techniques today?*

We do not walk and live with our learners as Jesus did. How then, can we teach 24/7? We can encourage learning throughout the week by the teaching approaches we use in our sessions together. Another way is by setting expectations for our learners. People today want expectations. The church has fallen in this area the past thirty years. In fact we have in many churches taken the opposite approach. "Don't ask them to do anything, we don't want to run them off." Set expectations for your learners. Not reading expectations—"be sure to read your Bible and your lesson for next week," these too often fall on deaf ears—but practice expectations. Challenge your learners to find ways to put to use the principles and truths discussed today into practice this coming week. No lesson is complete without a challenge. If your listeners are not challenged they cannot learn. Teach for life-change learning. Teach for transformation.

Some of the approaches or techniques used by Jesus during his ministry years are: 1) Discovery learning - leading His learners in self-discovery of how truths apply to each one individually and corporately. 2) Object lessons - using objects common and familiar to his listeners. 3) Illustrations and parables - stories, examples, and comparisons relational to His listeners. 4) Teachable Moments - ready to take advantage of a situation or need as it arose. 5) Practice - Jesus gave His learners time and opportunities to practice what they had learned. 6) Questions—Jesus used questions to activate higher-order thinking.

DISCOVERY LEARNING

First, let's look at *discovery learning*. We discussed discovery learning as a natural learning ability in chapter two. It is only appropriate that Jesus use a God-given instinctive ability to assist His listeners in the learning process. Since it is a natural, God-given, instinctive learning ability, we should employ it. Jesus did. Jesus used discovery learning throughout His ministry. He still uses it today. Let's look at some of

Jesus' Approach to Learning

these experiences as recorded in the gospels.

Think of Peter. Any discovery learning experiences come to mind? Because of Peter's personality, Jesus used discovery learning with him on several occasions. The account of Jesus walking on the water is recorded in three of the gospels including Matthew 14: 22-36. Did Peter learn by discovery that evening? Yes He did. And we can learn from those same events as well. I believe that Peter first learned that by being obedient to Jesus, supernatural things could be accomplished in and through natural circumstances. When Peter stepped out of the boat something happened that no man had ever seen or accomplished before or since.

Peter also had another discovery learning experience that evening. Peter discovered that the very second he took his eyes off of Jesus, he could no longer accomplish what he was able to accomplish when He was focused on Christ. When we teach this story, we must teach both sides of the truth presented. We can do all things through Christ. However, we must remember that it is the "through Christ" that makes it possible. I do not believe for Peter that the second half of this truth became concrete until after Christ's resurrection.

FREEZE FRAME

Had Jesus stood in the boat and lectured the disciples on how they could do all things through Him, would the lesson have made a life-changing impact as it did the way Jesus taught it? People learn best when they discover answers for themselves. What reasons can be presented to support this statement?

It is true that people learn best when they discover answers for themselves. In a lecture or monologue style teaching setting, the learner's thinking is not challenged. If the thinking - thought processes - are not employed, true learning cannot take place. Using learning methods to stimulate the thought processes allow the cognitive intelligence to stimulate the Limbic system of the brain. The Limbic system is the functioning unit of the brain, which processes and controls multifaceted behavior such as processing information, emotions, memory storage and recall. Allowing the learner to actively engage the thought processes in the teaching/learning session employs the learning portion of the brain — the Limbic system. As we discussed in chapter two, discovery learning is a natural ability and the main learning style in the first five years of a person's life - the most formidable learning years of our lives.

FREEZE FRAME

Read the following scriptures and identify what was the discovery in these learning experiences.
Matthew 19:16-26, Matthew 26:69-75,
Matthew 12:9-13, Matthew 14:15-21, and John 11.

Matthew 19:16-26 relates the story of the rich young ruler. The young man was wealthy and also apparently knowledgeable. Understanding the principle that learning builds upon learning, Jesus shared the truths of scripture with the young ruler. The young man stood with pride until Jesus shared with him that

Jesus' Approach to Learning

he needed to go and sell all that he had and give to the poor and then follow Jesus. Scriptures tell us at this point the young man went away sorrowful. Jesus knew not only the knowledge level of His listener, He also knew (perceived) the treasures of his heart. The man could not part with his material wealth. In the end it would be the weight around his neck, which pulled him down into hell. The discovery called for too great a sacrifice for the rich young ruler.

Jesus also took this opportunity to allow a discovery learning experience for His disciples. Read verses 24-26. The question raised by the disciples is, "Who then can be saved?" A study of the verse shows that in our current day vernacular it could read, "How then, can anyone be saved?" Witnessing the exchange with the rich young ruler, the disciples were prompted to higher-order thinking. They were ready for Jesus to help them in understanding. Had Jesus lectured His disciples on the matter, the opportunity for discovery would not have been availed. Discovery learning places the emphasis on learning not teaching.

OBJECT LESSONS

A second approach to learning that Jesus used was *object lessons*. Jesus used objects and story subjects that were familiar to his learners. Jesus used boats, fish, fig trees, oil, nets, wine, water, bread, seeds, and grain. Jesus always met the people, His learners, where they were at both physically and spiritually. Why use object lessons? By using object lessons, Jesus demonstrated that effective learning builds upon what the learner already knows.

We know what a boat is and what fish are today. And we could use many variations of boat and fish object lessons to help our learners apply Bible truths today. However, in Jesus' day, boats and fish were as common as McDonalds and Burger King are today and as essential as grocery stores. We can use the same objects Jesus did in His teaching. However, I believe the point of Jesus' teachings using object lessons, was relevancy. Relevancy for His learners. Yes, we know what boats and fish are. But, what lights went on in your head when you read the words McDonalds and Burger King in the above sentence? McDonalds is everywhere. There is nothing I could have said about fish or boats that would have triggered the same understanding in most adults living in America today.

FREEZE FRAME

What are objects you could use today that are common to those you teach? What are the fish, boats, seeds, and grain in your learner's lives?

Objects to be used in teaching will vary with the ages of learners. Object lessons for teenagers can include driver's licenses, name brand tennis shoes, contemporary music groups, pizza, and computerized games. Not too many senior adults would relate to any of those as object lessons, however. In the preschool area alone, the objects used vary greatly between a one-year-old and a five-year-old. While contemplating objects to be used

Jesus' Approach to Learning

consideration must be given to the relevancy of your learners.

As Christian educators it is important that we learn to use object lessons that are relevant to our listeners. Learning builds upon learning. The human learning system is able to take something that we already know - something that has been placed in our long-term memory - relate it to what we are being presented, make an emotional connection to the advanced concept and store it in our long-term memory. This is learning that brings about life-change.

One Sunday while teaching a class of adults in their fifties, I carried in a small flowering plant and a cup of water. We were studying Psalm 104. The truth I was wanting to teach is that God controls all things including the rains so that everything on the mountains and in the valleys get the amount of water and nutrients needed. I lifted the plant in one hand and the cup of water in the other and began pouring. "As the holder of this cup, I control how much water the plant gets." I stated. "If I withhold the water, the plant will eventually die. If I give it too much water it will die as well." About this time a gentleman from across the room said, "Yeah, and if you keep watering it from the top like that you're going to kill it, too. Those plants are to be watered from the bottom."

I took my unexpected cue and immediately held the cup of water under the planter. "Yes," I said, "But I haven't found a way to get the water through the bottom of this plastic container." Following a short pause I sat the cup of water down and lifted the plant out of the planter revealing a second planter inside the first one. The plant was actually in a drinking planter (one with holes in the bottom to allow the roots to drink water from the outside planter). The room then filled with "Aha's." Placing the plant back inside the planter I stated, "You did not know about the second planter, or that I was pouring the water beside it and into the bottom of the outside planter."

The learners could not see that I was actually doing what they had been telling me I needed to do, water the plant from the bottom. However, once I showed them the second planter and where the water was actually going, lights began to go off in their heads. One of the learners blurted out, "That's how God works in and around us. He provides all that we need even though we can't see all that is going on to make those provisions." Bingo! The object lesson had gone full circle and the revelation of the truth had been grasped. I did not have to prompt the revelation at all. I reinforced the learning experience immediately turning attention back to the scripture beginning in verse 10. The object lesson was a much greater success in teaching that morning than I had anticipated. It was successful because it was relational to the learners present that day.

Holding the plant up in class activated the recall of every person in the room. Some knew what type of plant was being displayed. Further examination revealed what was actually taking place — proper

Jesus' Approach to Learning

watering of the plant. Tying this to the truth brought about the "aha" moment.

You can use object lessons every session to help your learners connect to the truths being taught. Learning builds upon learning. Object lessons assist your learners in the learning process by motivating them to probe the 'how' questions. How does this relate to me? How does this relate to scripture and my spiritual life? Probing the 'how' questions prompts discovery learning as well as building upon the learner's prior learning. Starting with the learners context, prior knowledge and experience, emphasizes learning, not teaching.

It is easy to understand how object lessons use the Limbic system of the brain to process learning as explained in the section on discovery learning earlier in this chapter. When an object is seen for the first time the image is stored in memory cells of the brain. When the object is sighted again the image is recalled from its memory storage. A truth or experience being illustrated using the object is then attached to the image and stored along with the original image using the brain's Limbic system. This is how learning builds upon learning.

FREEZE FRAME

In the scriptures listed below, what are the objects Jesus uses to teach and what is the truth being conveyed? What impact does it have on his listeners? What impact would it have on you? Matthew 9:16-17, Matthew 19:24-26, Luke 7:36-48, John 4:6-26, John 3:1-8.

The gospels are filled with accounts of Jesus using object lessons to teach his listeners. However, object lessons are not only confined to Jesus' teaching in the Bible. The Old and New Testament are filled with object lessons. Jeremiah 18:2-4 is an object lesson. It is given to us as an illustration. But, God gave it to Jeremiah as an object lesson.

> *"Go down to the potter's house, and there I will give you my message. Then I went down to the potter's house and saw him working at the wheel. But the pot he was shaping from the clay was marred in his hands; so the potter formed it into another pot, shaping as it seemed best to him."*

God could have caused Jeremiah to learn the truth in any way he chose. God created Jeremiah, and He knew the power of the object lesson. God used Jeremiah's instinctive, God-given learning ability to produce learning that would create behavioral life-change. Today, as we read these verses, we clearly see the imagery and implications of the story and understand the practical application of the truth that we are as clay in the Master potter's hands. The truth and its application are comprehended today, several thousand years later, because God used an object lesson that He knew would still be universal in our present age.

Objects and illustrations allow learners to use natural and instinctive learning abilities. Learning builds upon learning.

Jesus' Approach to Learning

ILLUSTRATIONS, STORIES AND PARABLES

Another of Jesus' approaches to learning is *illustrations* and *stories* or *parables*. Jesus used illustrations not for the sake of filling time, or getting a laugh. I believe He has a sense of humor and told humorous stories. Yet, all of His illustrations, stories, and parables were delivered with the power to change lives. Illustrations entice the thought process by enlisting the brain to recall imagery from its storage cells. As we learned with object lessons the new information, truths, and applications can now be attached to these images and stored for learning that causes life-change.

Let's look at Matthew 16:2-4. Being approached by the Pharisee's, Jesus uses an illustration to create learning, not only for the Pharisee's but for His followers as well.

> *He (Jesus) replied, "When evening comes, you say, 'It will be fair weather, for the sky is red,' and in the morning, 'Today it will be stormy, for the sky is red and overcast.' You know how to interpret the sky, but you cannot interpret the signs of the times. A wicked and adulterous generation looks for a miraculous sign, but none will be given it except the sign of Jonah."Jesus then left them and went away.*

Jesus uses an illustration that all of His listeners would understand and relate to. It is an illustration that probes the thought processes. Reading this passage today, we stop to think of the illustration and the parallels of the morning and evening skies. We contemplate the different skies and the hues. In our mind's eye we recall the calming peace of a crimson evening sky. Why do we recall this scene in terms of calming, peaceful, and warm? It is because the crimson evening sky has been attached to a warm and pleasant emotion. The emotional tie is what has locked this into our long-term memory. The same is true with the vision of an angry red morning sky.

We relate that sky to a bad climatic condition, perhaps a destructive storm. Even if we have never personally experienced a stormy red clouded morning, the illustration painted by Jesus pulls together the two images of a clouded morning sky and a storm. Everyone has these two images stored in their long-term memory. The illustration unites the two images and demonstrates a distinction between this image and the one of the evening sky. Upon laying His foundation with the illustration, Jesus is able to impart the needed truth. The illustration calls upon the prior learning experience. The relation of the truth to the prior learning is the newly acquired learning experience. Learning builds upon learning.

Illustrations and stories are good learning approaches. Stories can be first person, second person, or parable in nature and content. First person is - a speaker relating a story, about himself. Second person is - a story related about someone else. The speaker is not in the story. A parable is a story (true or fictional) relating a moral or religious lesson.

Jesus' Approach to Learning

Many preachers, teachers, and speakers today, including myself, use first person stories. I have always considered these to be an effective means of communicating my message. However, I heard someone speaking on this issue a few years ago. He said Jesus used stories and illustrations throughout His ministry years. Yet, He never used first person stories or illustrations. You be the judge on whether or not to use first person in your teaching.

Jesus used stories throughout His ministry. The most common type He used was parables. Again, the Master Teacher was the Master at using parables. In some cases Jesus used more than one parable to illustrate the truth. This is the case in Matthew 13: 44-46. In these three short verses Jesus told two parables with equal significance concerning the kingdom of heaven. In fact, chapter 13 has no fewer than seven parables concerning the kingdom of heaven.

In my opinion one of the greatest parables for our learning is the parable of the Sower (Matt. 13: 1-8). Read this parable as a teacher. You are the Sower (farmer). The subject matter of your teaching is the seed. Your listeners represent the different types of ground.

FREEZE FRAME

In the scenario described above, how much of your seed is falling on good soil? How much is taking root? You will know by the changed lives of your learners.

Illustrations, stories, and parables should be

used to draw your listeners in to apprehension of the truth, just as the aroma of someone grilling draws you to food and the dinner table. Illustrations and parables should not be used as time filler. Rather, they should be used to bring your listeners to a point of awareness of prior learning and application of the truth being related at the present time. Emplacement of these two together will occur using the emotion of the prior learning or newly attached emotion which will reveal a future benefit for retaining this learning experience in the brain's information reserve.

Illustrations promote stimulation of the thought processes within the brain. If the thought processes can be activated, learning is likely to occur. Attaching a principle or truth to a recalled particle of information gives birth to new learning substance. Illustrations, stories, and parables use prior learning to create changed lives. Here, the emphasis is placed upon learning not teaching. Learning builds upon learning.

Teachable Moments

Jesus was great with all of his teaching methods. One that strikes me most and I really admire was his readiness to always take advantage of *teachable moments*. Jesus knew when his listeners were ripe for learning. I personally believe some of the greatest lessons Jesus taught were at these special moments.

Freeze Frame

Think of Jesus asleep at sea during the raging storm. What was the teachable moment?

Jesus' Approach to Learning

The woman caught in adultery. Who learned in that situation? The story of the woman caught in adultery reveals learning took place in the lives of not only the Pharisees but also the woman, the disciples, and the onlookers. In your opinion what was the incurred learning by each of these groups of people?

Raising Lazarus from the dead provided a great teaching moment. And it started four days prior to Lazarus' resurrection. As in several of Jesus' parables, there is more than one lesson to be learned from this teachable moment. Over the years I have heard and read many preachers and teachers as they have taught from this scripture (John 11: 1-44). In most cases the lesson conveyed is that the power of Jesus is greater than death. He can bring someone back to life from the dead. This line of thought may be teaching but it does not lend itself to learning.

To teach that Jesus has power over death is merely teaching fact. We do a grave injustice to God's word when we only teach the facts. The Bible was not given to us for facts and figures or as a history book. Facts alone do not commission learning. Facts alone cannot bring about life change.

> **FREEZE FRAME**
>
> *Stop now and read John 11:1-44 before reading the next paragraphs.*

Jesus used this teachable moment to give his learners something far greater than a substantiated fact. I can see Jesus sitting and teaching with people seated all around Him. Perhaps a child in His lap and several at His feet. In the middle of His teaching two messengers come to him and say, "Lord, behold the one you love is sick." Jesus replies, "The sickness is not unto death. No, it is for God's glory so that God's Son may be glorified through it." As soon as He has finished those words, Jesus turns back to the children and the business at hand, as not to give the messengers another thought. Verse six says that even though He loved Lazarus and his sisters very much, He stayed where He was two more days.

Verse 14 gives the first key to unlocking the truth Jesus is trying to convey to his disciples and to Lazarus' sisters. Verses 17-34 tell of Jesus' conversations first with Martha, then Mary. Both conversations are very similar. While Martha gives lip service to the Lord in verse 22 and 25, she does not understand the full implication of what Jesus is telling her. Even in verse 39 Martha cannot fathom what Jesus is about to do.

Mary, Martha, and the disciples had seen Jesus heal sick persons before. Mary and Martha's faith was strong enough to know Jesus could heal their brother. They were about the urgent. Jesus, on the other hand, was always about the important. Jesus was ready to take His learners to a new level in their faith journey. To the sisters, what was important was the urgency that Jesus 'come quickly' to heal their brother before death. To Jesus the important matter was to raise their plain of faith by overpowering death. It is the cognitive awareness of the truth that allows true learning to transpire.

Jesus' Approach to Learning

Could not the same learning occur when we see a magician push several swords through a wooden box housing his assistant? What is the difference? The magician's assistant walks out of her believed tomb. Lazarus walked out of his tomb. We know one is an illusion. Could the difference be the love that Jesus displayed for Lazarus, Mary, and Martha? Love is an emotion, is it not? Is there a link between life-changing learning and emotion? Yes, a direct connection as we have discussed in earlier chapters. It is the emotion that ties the benefit of the truth to the prior experience, which causes life-changing learning.

As Christian educators we need to be ready for teachable moments, not only in the classroom on Sunday mornings (or whenever your class meets). We need to be ready and aware of our learner's readiness to learn, whether in the parking lot on Sunday afternoon, at the ballpark on Thursday evening or at the class cookout on Saturday. As Thom and Joani Schultz of Group Publishing put it, "When Jesus observed people engaged in a captivating activity, He knew they were ready to learn."[4] And He capitalized on the opportunity. We can learn to take advantage of teachable moments from Jesus' example. Begin by accepting that our learners will learn little or nothing if they are uninterested or bored. When they are captivated or fascinated by something, they are already learning and positioned for increased learning.

PRACTICE

Practice makes perfect. The absolute most

dependable mode of learning to use to insure that a lesson will adhere in a learner's life is to allow your learners to put the lesson into practice. Few lessons stick without putting those lessons into practice. You can lecture on riding a bicycle, but if you never allow your listener to practice, they will never be able to ride. Think about it; ninety-five percent of what you have learned has remained with you because in some way you put it into practice. Phone numbers - you remember the ones you have dialed. Which numbers are easiest for you to remember? The ones you dial most often. The more you use something or put it into practice, the more easily it is recalled.

I have heard for years that we learn by repetition. There is truth to this statement. However, I believe many educators hold a misconception of the truth. The misconception is that we must keep repeating ourselves. "If I say it enough times, eventually some of it will sink in and my listeners will learn." The results would be similar to pouring oil over the outside of your car's engine with the expectation of some of the oil eventually soaking in and lubricating the necessary internal parts. It won't happen! Oral repetition may cause a guilt trip occasionally. Nonetheless, your chances of being struck by lightning are probably greater than causing life-changing learning by oral repetition.

The truth in the thought - we learn by repetition - is in the recurrence of acting on the principle or truth of the lesson. It is being able to apply the truth - to put it into practice. I have read the statement,

Jesus' Approach to Learning

"Tell me and I will forget. Show me and I may remember. Involve me and I will understand." If every educator, preacher and teacher could grasp the truth in this statement, our education systems, religious and secular, would be revolutionized. I do not believe there is a more potent statement or paragraph in this book than the previous two sentences!

The gospels often record citations of Jesus permitting His learners to practice what He had been teaching. Matthew 10 and Mark 6 give record of Jesus sending the disciples out to practice what they had observed and learned under his instruction. Remember the rich young ruler, Jesus instructed him in what to do, then challenged him to sell all his possessions. What happened? Was the intended lesson a failure? The young man apparently learned. His short-coming was in his unwillingness to accept Jesus' teaching in full application to his life. When we allow our learners opportunities to practice we must give them permission to come back with results other than our one specific success-oriented expectation. They may fail. Yet, many of our most well learned lessons come from so-called failures.

Jesus taught His disciples about betrayal, then gave the twelve time to practice their devotion. When we think of Jesus being betrayed, we think of Judas. But what of the other disciples? Did they not betray Him on the night of His apprehension and trial? Not one of them stood up for Him. Peter was the only one who followed - at a great distance. And three times that night he denied even knowing Jesus. What did the practice do for Peter the night of Jesus' trial? I believe when the cock crowed upon his third denial of knowing Christ the lesson he learned was forever inveterated in Peter's mind. At that very instant everything Christ had told Peter about betrayal and loyalty, flashed before Peter's eyes. The scriptures tell us that Peter went out and wept. Why?

The burden of truth had pierced his heart at the very moment Peter gave his third denial. He was allowed to practice his loyalty. The lesson he learned was not what Peter expected. Many times our best learning comes from apparent failures during practice. However, if you learn from any situation it is not a failure. As long as you get up, dust yourself off, and learn from the encounter, then the experience was not a failure but a success. Remember, true learning brings about behavioral life-change. If a change has been made, our efforts will concentrate on not allowing the same results. God used Peter's denial experience to enforce the truth and law of loyalty. The searing of this lesson was so intense that it was Peter who would lead the disciples and the early church in its infancy and early persecution.

FREEZE FRAME

Unscramble this word - evnsrta - before reading further.

The absolute most dependable mode of learning to use to insure that a lesson will adhere in a learner's life is to allow your learners to put the lesson into practice. Allow your learners time in class to

Jesus' Approach to Learning

brainstorm how they will practice the learned truth in the week ahead. If time permits have the class form groups of two or three and practice on each other. Practicing the practice promotes repetition and repetition promotes learning - life-changing learning. Practice results in genuine learning. Teach for life change. Teach to bear fruit.

> **FREEZE FRAME**
>
> *The word in the previous Freeze Frame is servant. Are you a better servant for unscrambling the word? Will members of your class become better servants by you standing in front of them and lecturing them in servanthood? Or asking them to help prepare a meal for a family in need? Practice results in genuine learning.*

Chapter Four

The Art of the Question

One of the superlative teaching techniques proven throughout history is the use of questions. Inquiry through question is one of the greatest means of communication and learning known to man. With a question you can: 1) gather information, 2) embark on a quest of a person's prior knowledge, 3) make a statement soliciting your listeners approval, and 4) promote higher level thinking.

More than twenty years ago as I entered the world of sales, one of the first things we were taught in people skills was the use of questions. It was not an in-depth study or lesson. Yet, it was enough to rev up my thought processes. I quickly became a student of the question. In the ensuing years I have read and studied about questions. I have studied the various types of questions, how to employ and deploy questions, as well as the wording of questions. I deliberated and practiced different delivery techniques, voice inflection, and the emotion of a question. One great lesson I learned early on is, "It is not what you say so much as how you say it."

From our early childhood days most of us have learned to use questions to gather information. "But why, Mom?" or "What if I ...Dad?" "How does this work?" "What makes the thingamabob jiggle and the whatchamacallit squeak?" We go through life using the question this way. But, when God fabricated the question He created so much more than information gathering.

In education we can use the question to gain an understanding of our learners' prior learning. Whether in religious or secular education, the question can be used to evaluate a person's prior knowledge or progress. Jesus used this line of questioning. In Matthew 16:13-16 we see one such instance:

> *When Jesus came to the region of Caesarea Philippi, He asked His disciples, "Who do people say the Son of Man is?"*
> *"Some say John the Baptist, others say Elijah, and still others Jeremiah or one of the prophets."*
> *"But what about you? He asked, "Who do you say I am?"*
> *Simon Peter answered, "You are the Christ, the Son of the Living God."*

The Art of the Question

Jesus' first question was a query of the disciples reaction to what other people were saying. What is the word on the street, the scuttlebutt so to speak? Jesus knew what others were saying. He used this question to get a picture of the disciples reaction to what others were saying. This is a good learning tool for an educator. Human Resource professionals use this type of question in personnel interviews every day. Perhaps in an employment interview you have been asked a question similar to this; "Why should I hire you over anyone else applying for the job?" These are used as reaction questions. Police and court authorities use this line of questioning as well. It can serve the educator as a barometer for learning.

Jesus' next question is to ascertain the learning level of the disciples. "*But what about you, who do you say I am?*" The answer given to the first question was not from persons whom had eaten, slept, and drank—lived daily—with Jesus. They had not been with Jesus in the inner circle. These were people who had seen outward manifestations and heard portions of His teachings. To answer the second question the way he did, Simon Peter must have had a life-changing experience. True learning is about life-change.

The disciples could have said, "We agree, you are someone special to God. You say you are the Son of God and we think there is certainly some possibility there." But they did not. In fact, Simon Peter's is the only answer recorded. Jesus tells him in the very next verse (17), "*Blessed are you Simon, son of*

Jonah, for this was not revealed to you by man, but by my Father in heaven." Peter's answer was the result of a revelation of true life-changing learning. Learn to use questions to assist you in understanding your learners prior knowledge.

Statement Questions

You can also use questions to make almost any statement you desire. I enjoy using this and teaching people about it. Salesmen and women use this all day long. In fact someone has probably used it with you today, haven't they? Parents use this form with their children, don't they? Sometimes, children use this line of questioning with their parents, wouldn't you say? It happens all day long, doesn't it? I've been using it the last five statements I have made, haven't I? I sometimes use this in conferences and seminars and after about the fourth question, smiles and sheepish grins begin to appear on faces around the room. Then, when I make an assessment like the fifth question/statement, everyone realizes what has happened and lights start going on in heads all around the room. Another "aha!" moment. Teaching can be fun and learning should be fun, interesting and relative.

Did Jesus use questions like this in His teachings? He sure did. Let's look at Matthew 18:33. In His parable of the unforgiving servant, Jesus uses this question of the master, *"Shouldn't you have had mercy on your fellow servant just as I had on you?"* Is there a statement made in this sentence? It is clearly a statement placed in question form just like the ones parents use

The Art of the Question

with children. Earlier in that same chapter, the parable of The Lost Sheep, Jesus sets the stage with a question, then forms the entire parable into a question.

What do you think? If a man owns a hundred sheep, and one of them wanders away, will he not leave the ninety-nine on the hills and go to look for the one that wandered off?

What an impact this has on the learning process. Jesus not only turned His opening statement into a question. He prefaces it with a question, "*What do you think?*" That may look like a question at first sight but look at it again. "*What do you think?*" Is it a question or a decree? He is verbally directing His listeners to think. His statement is, 'To fully understand this you must think.' Not surface level thinking. You must employ your higher-level thinking. He knew his listeners could have given a quick and superficial answer (they could have been willing to give the 'pat' answer). As a Christian let me encourage you to do as Jesus did. Stir those thought processes.

In verse 49 of Luke chapter 2, Jesus poses this statement as a question to His mother and Joseph; "*Didn't you know I had to be in my Father's house?*" I told you children use this line of questioning with their parents. Perhaps they have learned it from Jesus? At the age of twelve Jesus was making a statement demonstrating His understanding of who He was and His life purpose while on earth.

Another example is found in Mark 7:18, "*Don't

you see that nothing that enters a man from the outside can make him unclean?" Here Jesus is making a statement of denotation and in the following verses He gives clarification of the statement and the illustration in verses 14-15. In Mark 11:17 Jesus quotes Isaiah 56:7. However, He changes the statement to a question. *"My house will be called a house of prayer? ...But you have made it a den of robbers."*

Again in Mark 12:10 (KJV), Jesus forms a question by quoting scripture. Once again it is following a parable and used to solidify a truth.

"And have you not read this scripture; The stone which the builders rejected is become the head of the corner: This was the Lord's doing, and it is marvelous in our eyes?"

While this line of questioning does not normally bring about learning, they can be used to set the stage for a learning experience. In Mark 11:17 Jesus used scripture quotation to impact the learning experience in His next statement. In Mark 12:10 He formed a question from scripture to expose the Pharisees. Jesus used these 'set-up' questions throughout His ministry. Using questions to set the stage for a learning experience focuses on a known fact or learned experience to prepare your learners for a new learning experience. It could be said that using these questions is similar to creating your own teachable moment.

The Art of the Question

OPEN ENDED QUESTIONS

Another form of questioning encourages higher-order thinking. Higher-order thinking generates learning. Learning results in life-change. To promote higher-level thinking educators must use open-ended questions. Many educators use closed-ended questions and expect learning, where it cannot transpire. A closed-ended question is one that can be answered with a definite, factual answer. Questions exacting yes and no answers are closed-ended. In many churches and Christian education settings the banter is to give the "pat" answer if asked a question. What is the "pat" answer? Yes, no, or Jesus. One of the three is bound to be what the teacher is looking for.

The reason this thought is so widespread is Christian educators for years have used only closed-ended questions. In preparing for a class, session, or conference I always try to avoid using closed-ended questions. Today, if a question comes to mind, it is normally an open-ended question. This comes through years of training my thought process to stimulate higher-order thinking in myself as well as my learners. Should a closed-ended question come to mind, I rethink it. How can I reword this to stimulate the thinking processes in my learners?

Closed-ended questions shut down any possibility of creative thinking. As Christian educators we must remove the closed-ended question from our repertoire. It not only does not promote learning, in many cases it will squelch the potentiality of learning. Some teachers and educators use closed-ended questions and refuse to use open-ended questions for different reasons. Those reasons usually include 1) fear of losing control of the teaching process, 2) fear of not knowing the one definite answer, 3) fear of not being able to deliver all they have prepared. Did you notice anything in common about those three reasons? All three evolve from fear. They are a fear of the unknown.

Educator's fear using open-ended questions because they do not know the power locked inside each one. Delivering one open-ended question can produce more learning than multiple hours of lecture or monologue. As one person responds to the question, others in the room are forced into higher-order thinking. There may not be one right answer. There may be several avenues to the right answer. Some of those avenues you, the educator, may never have entertained. Utilizing open-ended questions enables the Holy Spirit to use others in the teaching/learning process.

As each response is given to an open-ended question every person in the room must mentally react. How is this done? It is as we have discussed earlier. As a response is given, each person must call on prior learning experiences to assess the information being offered. Then when a truth is exposed in a response, a reconfiguration or reformulation of the prior learning along with the current experience occurs which will bring about true life-change learning.

As we look into the gospels, we see Jesus used

open-ended questions quite often in His teaching. Let's look again at Matthew 19 and the story of the rich young ruler. In verse 17 Jesus says, "*Why do you ask me about what is good?*" With this question Jesus is actuating higher-order thinking. All who are listening must call upon prior learning to contemplate what is 'good.'

The King James Version of Luke records Jesus using no less than sixty-eight open-ended questions to promote higher-level thinking in the learning process during his ministry. Many of Jesus' other questions quoted in Luke, though they might be borderline open-ended, require higher-order thinking, as well. Very seldom did Jesus pose a question, which did not promote higher-order thinking.

Great teaching is recorded throughout the gospels. Chapter 12 in the book of Matthew illustrates some of Jesus' great teaching utilizing questions. In verse 10 Jesus answers the question of His accusers with a question. Jesus used this technique several times with the Pharisee's and others. He used it to turn the tables when they tried to trap Him. He also uses it as a learning tool. As Christian educators we must be proficient in the use of and willing to employ this approach in our teaching.

When someone asks a question of you, do you immediately and automatically give the answer or your opinion and belief? This is not always the best course to take. How is the learning process employed in this situation? Most times it is not employed. We do not give our listeners' time or opportunity to exercise the learning process. We can give definitive answers and absolutes. We can teach the Bible as history and information, facts and figures. But if we want spiritual transformation to take place in the lives of our listeners, we must allow them to become learners. Many believers walk in and out of churches today because we have not allowed or challenged them to become learners. When we do not allow our listeners to become learners, we are guilty of not allowing them to practice James 1:22 (KJV); *"Be ye doers of the Word, and not hearers only."* Empower your listeners to become learners. Teach for life-change.

Enable the Learning Process

When asked a question, do not always give an immediate answer. A well-prepared teacher (leader and guide) will assist the student in applying the learning process. It is not a sign of ignorance or unpreparedness to pause before answering. You should pause before continuing. A simple five-second pause will cause the cognitive thought processes of your listeners to kick into gear. People will begin to consider the posed question. You, as the leader, should contemplate not how the question can best be answered, but how learning can best take place. Instead of immediately giving your learners the answer, help them in the discover-learning process. The lesson to be learned is more likely to be retained.

Your point of convergence when structuring questions to be used in class should be the under-

The Art of the Question

standing of the principle, truth, or concept being discussed within the learners' context. Questions such as: "What is meant by this?" or "What does this mean to you, today?" "How has God worked in your life, in this respect?" "How can you apply this in your world this coming week?"

As a word of caution let me say it is better to offer your question to the class as a whole and expect individuals to offer responses rather than singling out one person to answer. People do not like to be 'put on the spot' by a teacher asking them pointedly. Adults especially are more apt to respond if not singled out. Also posing a question to an individual does not allow that person to devote his/her thought processes solely to the question. The called upon individual is forced into a bi-thought process. While trying to contemplate a response to the question, the subconscious has also enacted the thought processes. 'It is me everyone is looking at and waiting on. I must give the right answer.' The subconscious will distract the person and the higher-order thinking needed to process the information correctly for true life-changing learning. Even after attention is turned away from that individual, he/she will reconsider the answer given and whether or not it was received as intended.

Questions are a very important part of the learning process. Without questions it is arduous to promote higher-order thinking which produces learning. Incorporating questions in your teaching process does not necessarily guarantee learning will occur. Incorporating the right types of questions, however, will certainly assist in and encourage the learning process. Questions should be used to stimulate the learning processes of the mind. Questions are universal to all learning styles.

We could devote an entire book on the use of questions in the teaching/learning process. In the last few pages you have been exposed to an overview of a few ways to use questions. This is not an exhaustive study of questions. Nor is it an exhaustive investigation of the techniques Jesus employed in utilizing questions in His teachings. Jesus used rhetorical questions. He used questions to reveal motives.

If I can encourage you to begin with only one principle explored in this book, it would be to become a student of the question. Study the use of questions by other speakers and master teachers. Proper employment of questions not only comprises the wording, it also encompasses voice tone and inflection, body language, eye contact and the emotion of the question.

One other critical factor many teachers and speakers neglect is - For every question you ask, you must allow time and freedom for your listeners to answer. I have sat in many classes where the listeners were guided toward and aimed in the direction of a very timely and needful learning experience, only to have the teacher cruise right past the learning experience at Mach I speed. Questions posed by the teacher were answered by the teacher without giving

The Art of the Question

the listeners a chance to react. The listeners never had a chance to catch the desired truth or principle. Where there is no opportunity for the stimulation of higher-order thinking, there is no learning. Many times one open-ended question is all that is required to allow your listeners to achieve the learning experience. Rick Yount, associate professor at Southwestern Baptist Theological Seminary says, "My rule is simple: Never ask a question unless you want a learner to answer it."[5]

In preparing for each teaching session endeavor to place as many questions in your teaching as possible. Alter the wording of each question in various ways. With each rewording, ask the question in your mind and mentally prepare how each version will be received, perceived and answered by each person in class. Remember, not every person will be comfortable answering verbally. You must ask yourself how this question will affect each person that might be in attendance. What wording of this question will best promote higher-order thinking to produce true life-changing learning? How will it change his and her life? How will it bring about life-change? How will it affect the way they relate to their coworkers, neighbors, family members, fellow students, and teammates?

Over the years it has been said that you cannot put a price on a good education. In many ways it is priceless. Jesus knew the value of a question. I believe if you asked Him, He would say you cannot put a value on the proper use of questions in the education setting. Proper lines of questioning promote higher-order thinking. Higher-order thinking produces true life-changing learning. The value of a question - priceless! This is teaching that bears fruit.

Chapter Five

Curriculum and Application Driven Teaching

To reach people today the curriculum used must actively engage the learners and promote higher-order thinking. We have looked at this in earlier chapters. Many Christian educators teach history and information. Most do this unknowingly. We teach the way we were taught. When choosing curriculum for your education setting ask yourself several questions about the curriculum. The first question to ask is, "Does this curriculum lend itself to life-changing learning or is it relating information, facts and figures?" Through the last several years I have examined curriculum from different publishers. Today there is a wide assortment of curriculum available from various publishers. Some denominations have their own writers and publishing houses. Some para-church groups write and print Bible study curricula. And there are independent publishers of Sunday School, and Bible study materials. Aside from these choices, a number of churches write their own Bible study curriculum.

Along with the variety of publishers comes a wide variation of curriculum as well. You can choose from doctrinally defined material specific to your denomination. You can purchase curriculum that teaches doctrine up to the point of crossing the line of any one or more denominations. An example of this would be baptism. While most Christian religions believe in and practice baptism there are certainly different views on baptism. In this case a denomination based publisher would discuss the doctrine and ordinance of baptism according to their beliefs. An independent publisher, on the other hand, would use scripture to provide the doctrinal basis for baptism without stating any particular methods or styles of baptism. This allows each church to adapt the material to their beliefs and practices on the ordinance of baptism.

Two more types of curriculum being produced are content-driven and application-driven. Today, many Christian publishers are turning to application-driven material, and for good reason. For years, much of the material written for Christian education was content-driven. While content-driven curriculum is notable, studies completed by secular and Christian researchers have proven time and time again, it does not lend itself to learning as well as application-driven curriculum. I believe there were several misconceptions that brought this type of teaching material (content-driven) to the forefront of Christian education. In this chapter we will take a look at some of these misperceptions.

Facts Don't Change Lives

The first misconception is *'We must get the facts out.'* While this may be true, facts do not change lives. It all goes back to the "We teach the way we were taught" syndrome. We were taught from a pedagogical style, one person stands in front of a group of learners and dispenses the required information. As we discussed in chapter one, being a dispenser of information, facts, and figures does not produce life-change learning. Merely dispensing information will no more guarantee learning than baiting a trap for bear in inner city Los Angeles will guarantee catching a bear.

One spring while living in rural Ohio, between the cities of Dayton and Cincinnati, my wife and I found our attic had become home to a mother raccoon and her litter of four. The mother raccoon was going out under the cover of darkness and returning with food for her little ones once they were big enough to eat. I decided the humane thing to do was trap the raccoons using tender traps and release them in a nearby state reserve. I borrowed a couple of traps and tried using cut apples and lettuce for bait. This was to no avail. I then learned a friend of mine had faced the same situation earlier that year. I called him up and found out that he used peanut butter on bread to trap the raccoon from his attic. The first try was successful. I had trapped all but one raccoon the first night.

You see, I had the trap and what I thought would be a result-producing bait. My deduction was that these raccoons were not used to human processed foods. My belief was they would be attracted to something they were used to in the wild, something natural, fruit and vegetables common to their environment. Yet there was no interest on their part for the fruit. However, when I put something in the trap that was appealing to the raccoons, almost instantly it brought about results. Though they had never had peanut butter, it was something they were willing to apply themselves for. They were willing to step out of their comfort zone and experience something new and different, rather than walking around it and ignoring it.

The peanut butter definitely brought about a life-change for the raccoons, especially the young ones. My experience with the raccoons is similar to the experience taking place in many Christian education settings every week throughout our country. The curriculum we use represents the trap. It is the tool we use to try to change the life-style of our learners represented here by the raccoons. Our goal is to move our learners from the attic to an area of life where they can be productive for God. The fruit and vegetables represent the delivery (teaching methods) we use as educators. We believe it is exactly what our listeners will respond to. As we examine the lives of our listeners, however, to our dismay we find they are not

Curriculum and Application Driven Teaching

responding at all. They are, in essence, walking right past our efforts to help them in their spiritual walk.

We need to find the peanut butter for our listeners. What will cause them to step out of their comfort zone and experience the next level of spiritual transformation? Over the past few years publishers of Christian education materials have been coming to some realizations and making strides to change their outlook on writing curriculum. It is not only a matter of getting the information out. To change lives curriculum must be relational, interesting, and applicable. You can have your attic covered with tender traps (the best theological material available), but without the means to allow and entice your listeners to apply themselves to the principle and the principles to their lives, they are empty tender traps - nothing more than information, facts and figures.

THE NEED FOR TEACHER TRAINING

A second misconception about content-driven curriculum has been, *'The teacher will be able to relate the material to his or her learners.'* This is a misperception that has taken me several years to come to grips with. Many teachers, i.e. Christian educators, do not know how to relate anything other than what is in print in front of them to their listeners. Albeit, most teachers can be trained. All that is required is a willing heart and a teachable spirit.

My wife was teaching fifth and sixth graders at a church where I was serving as Youth Pastor in the early nineties. It was her first year teaching and she was having difficulty with her lessons. I would periodically sit down and help her. When I sat down to look at the lesson, ideas and application began to leap off the page at me. I was glad to help Pam and thought the reason she could not ascertain teaching possibilities as easily as I could was perhaps due to her inexperience and the fact that she had not grown up in Bible study.

A few years later while I was serving as Minister of Education at another church, Pam again accepted teaching responsibilities in the fifth and sixth grade department. While making my rounds on Sunday morning, I noticed her class playing Bible games twenty minutes into the hour. I trust my wife and know that games are a real source of learning for grade school children. However, Pam expressed one day that she just could not get anything out of the lesson to last more than fifteen minutes for her class. She was getting frustrated with it.

Concerned that we might need to change curriculum, I decided to take her material and re-evaluate it. I began with the next week's lesson. To my surprise, within ten minutes I had made notes and comments, highlighted, underlined and scribbled in the margins enough teaching possibilities to last most of the teaching hour, and I had only focused on the first of three sets of scriptures for the day. My surprise had not come in what I had accomplished through my review of the curriculum. Rather, it was a much deeper realization.

That evening I realized not everyone in Christian education settings has the creative ability to construct

Curriculum and Application Driven Teaching

a life-changing application-driven lesson from material. It was also on that evening that I realized the need for teaching material for teachers. Proper training assisting them in delivering scriptural truths in ways to transform lives. That evening I was struck with the realization that Christian education had been failing in its intent and purpose for years, in part due to the lack of proper training for teachers. If we expect our foot soldiers (teachers) to be able to teach to change lives we must provide proper training.

Can you imagine how incompetent the United States Army would be if with every group of new recruits the instruction were; Select a leader from among yourselves. Here is the Army's operating manual. Train as your new leader instructs and be ready for battle in six weeks. We would not have much of an army, would we? This illustration seems rather trite and silly, yet, it is exactly how we recruit and treat Sunday school and Bible study teachers in most of our churches today.

We can take a lesson from the military here. The Army or other branches of our military forces have well-trained, qualified leaders in place to train new recruits. As Christian educators we have the responsibility to continually study and obtain ample training to be at our best in training others for life transformation. The military and any other career path you choose normally provides updated training throughout the course of your employment. The same is true with Christian education. In fact, our desire should be to continually strive to improve in our God-given abilities. This is our fulfillment of Philippians 2:12-13.

> *"Continue to work out your salvation with fear and trembling. For it is God who works in you to will and to act according to his good purpose."*

We receive our spiritual gifts and a full pardon from sin at the moment of salvation. However, God expects us to discover and continually develop those gifts and abilities as we pursue our spiritual journey. Verse 13 says He "*works in you.*" It does not say He worked in you. "*Works*" is present tense. God is working in us throughout all of our Christian life. As Christian educators, the development and use of our leadership and teaching abilities is the outward manifestation of God working in us. There is never a time to stop training and growing for the Lord.

While serving a church in Ohio in the latter 1990's, I had a gentleman and his wife, Woodrow and Geneva Wall, who attended every teacher training event in the church or promoted by the church. Mrs. Wall taught one of our women's classes and her husband was an associate teacher (substitute). In my five years at the church I only recall two or three events (out of approximately 50) they were not able to attend. To miss, they were either out of town of gravely ill. Why do the Wall's stick in my mind? Woodrow Wall was 82 years young when I left the church. Many times they would come out of a training session and comment, "It is the same things we've

Curriculum and Application Driven Teaching

heard for years, just put a different way." That being true, they continued to attend. Why? Because they were convicted it was their obligation as a teacher and their obligation to God and His scripture.

If we intend to impact our learners lives we must first impact our own lives. We are called to perpetually work to improve our abilities to insure we are teaching to change lives.

ENGAGING LISTENERS IN THE LEARNING PROCESS

A third misconception is *'As long as we provide the scripture basis, the Holy Spirit will do the rest.'* This is either spiritual immaturity or an excuse for laziness and fear. It is true the Holy Spirit is our teacher. However, God has called us to do a job. If your child or grandchild asks for cake, you do not hand them a plate with the raw ingredients - an egg, flour, sugar, oil and water - and say enjoy. You are the one with the knowledge that these must be combined correctly to create the desired out come. You combine the ingredients and place them in a heated oven. In a matter of minutes you experience the results as a cake is removed from the oven. The same is true with Christian education.

You study to learn the raw ingredients and the method of preparation. You cannot expect learning to occur any more than you would expect a child to eat the raw ingredients of a cake. The method of preparation is your delivery style. How will you deliver this truth (content) so that it is edible? You combine the ingredients - content, learner's context, and application - and place it in the oven—your learners' cognitive-processes. It is through the heat of the Holy Spirit that your properly mixed ingredients will rise and produce the desired outcome.

The book of Jeremiah focuses on God's plans for the nation of Israel. Throughout the book God's plans and provision for the Israelites are recorded. Crossing the Jordan River, the taking of Jericho, defeating their enemies, conquering the land. His provision always came as the Israelites stepped into action on their belief that God would provide. All of scripture is filled with God providing and fulfilling the need at hand as His people satisfied their obligation and stepped out in faith.

Peruse the gospels and try to list the number of times Jesus taught and brought about healing by requesting something of those receiving His instruction. Jesus required His listeners and learners to take part in the learning experience. We have looked at several of these in earlier chapters. Every time He asked a question He was inviting His listeners to engage in the learning experience. With each parable and illustration He spoke and with each object lesson he depicted, Jesus engaged his listeners in the education process. For some He required a physical response.

> *"But go, show yourself to the priest and offer the gift Moses commanded, as a testimony to them."* Matthew 8:4
> *"Rise, take up your bed and go home."* Matthew 9:6
> *"Go wash in the pool of Siloam."* John 9:7

Curriculum and Application Driven Teaching

The list goes on and on. Jesus engaged His learners in the education process and God expects no less from teachers and Christian educators today. The Word is His. He does not need nor does He desire us to share content only. He has called us to '*didasko*'—the act of causing our listeners to accept and assimilate. Your goal as a teacher should be to enable your listeners to accept and understand God's truths and to incorporate them into their daily lives.

> **FREEZE FRAME**
>
> *Stop and ask God to sear this next statement into your cognizance.*
>
> **"I must not expect God to do what He has called me to do in His power."**

WE'VE ALWAYS DONE IT THIS WAY

A fourth misconception about using content-driven material is, "*We've always done it this way.*" A sentence that normally follows this statement is; "*And it has worked for us so far.*" The misconception lies in the second statement. The question is, has it worked? What are the evidences of learning? How has the Holy Spirit manifested Himself through the teaching/learning process in your church or class in the last few years? The facts are content-driven curriculum does not yield life-changing learning—life transformation. What we think we are teaching and what they are actually learning are two vastly different things. Thom and Joani Schultz of Group Publishing, display this very well in their book "*Why*

Nobody Learns Much of Anything at Church: and How to Fix It." Group has invested great time and resources in research and continues to research these processes to further assist Christian educators in the teaching/learning process.

Bruce Wilkinson, President and founder of Walk thru the Bible, devotes a chapter to this in his book "*Seven Laws of the Learner*".[6] Realizing he was a content-driven teacher, Dr. Wilkinson did not want to believe the truth that through the ages the great "master teachers" were and are today application-driven, not content-driven. He sat out on a quest taking sermons and lessons of, first, his contemporaries Charles Swindoll, Charles Stanley and Howard Hendricks. His quest was to audit their teachings for content and application. Taking two different colored highlighter markers, Dr. Wilkinson and a coworker read through each sermon or lesson and highlighted with one color each statement that was content-oriented. With the other colored marker they highlighted each statement or phrase that appeared to be application. In his heart he wanted to disprove the application 'theory.' The sermons and teachings reviewed proved to be greater than 50% application. Next, he pursued some of Christianity's great teachers of times gone by. He analyzed men such as D.L. Moody, Jonathan Edwards, Charles Finney, Charles Spurgeon, John Wesley and more. The same results as before, everyone averaged between forty-five and seventy-five percent application.

He then checked the Bible—the New Testament. Romans is considered to be one of the heaviest content books of the New Testament. Dr. Wilkinson's findings—chapter by chapter - Romans is fifty percent application. Ephesians is fifty percent application. The book of James is eighty percent application. He also checked Jesus' teachings. Jesus' teachings are always greater in application than content. Jesus is the 'King of Application.' His teachings are almost always above seventy percent application and several that I have checked are greater than eighty percent application. Application-driven teaching changes lives. It worked for Jesus, and it works today as we allow Him to work through us by listening to the Holy Spirit.

Content vs Application

What is the difference between "content" and "application"? Content deals with information, facts, figures, knowledge, and material. Application, on the other hand, pertains to transformation, wisdom, and maturity. Notice application relates to transformation instead of information (facts and figures). Wisdom rather than knowledge is a quality of application. Knowledge is the gathering of information, facts and figures. Wisdom is the understanding of to what purpose the knowledge gained can and should be used. One last comparison to be made is that application bears upon maturity rather than material. Content can give you the substantive information, knowledge and material. Yet, without application, it is nothing more than stored trivia.

Along with the information, we must give our learners the means to use the information to transform —

change — their lives. In the process of imparting knowledge to our learners, we must strive to assist them in acquiring the wisdom of using the knowledge procured. As we transfer material to our learners we must advocate the advancement of their spiritual maturity.

> **FREEZE FRAME**
>
> *Look at Matthew 16:2-4. Underline the sentences or phrases that you consider content (what applies to information, facts, material). Circle the words, phrases or sentences you consider application (dealing with transformation, wisdom, and maturity).*

He replied, "When evening comes, you say, 'It will be fair weather, for the sky is red,' and in the morning, 'Today it will be stormy, for the sky is red and overcast.' You know how to interpret the appearance of the sky, but you cannot interpret the signs of the times. A wicked and adulterous generation looks for a miraculous sign, but none will be given it except the sign of Jonah."

There are seventy-three words in these verses. How many did you see as content and how many as application? I marked fifty-two words as application. That is seventy-one percent. Verses two and three are application-driven. Verse four is content-driven. I did not pull this teaching of Jesus out because it fit my statistics. After reading Dr. Wilkinson's work on Jesus' teachings, I did what

Curriculum and Application Driven Teaching

the Bible tells us to do. I went to the Word and began examining His teachings myself. I picked up a red-lettered edition and opened to this passage first. Not intentionally, it is the first red-lettered section I opened to. Needless to say, I was soon convinced. I trust you will do the same. I later examined a sample of my own teachings, two Sunday school lessons and a conference on teacher training. I was pleased and relieved to find my teachings were at least in the lower sixty-percentile range for application.

The Bible is our textbook and it provides our content. However, as we have just experienced it also provides application. The curriculum materials you choose should assist educators in moving God's truths and principles into practical application in the lives of their learners as well as their own lives. Curriculum that does not avail in providing life transformation should be avoided. It leads teachers into an information-dispensing trap.

Content-driven curriculum does not necessarily need to be taught as content-driven. In actuality, though, it is taught that way over ninety percent of the time in today's Christian education settings. The reason —most teachers do not know how to turn it into application. It requires a change in thinking, theory, preparation, and practice. For some teachers it is difficult. However, as I have watched teachers make the transition over the past few years, I believe each one of them would testify to the incremental progression of their teaching and the actual learning and life-change of their listeners.

Caution: Do not expect to see immediate life-change results. It will take time. After all, the teacher has in many cases been teaching a certain way for years. Teaching for life-change requires an adjustment on the part of the teachers and the learners as well. If they are use to a lecture or monologue-style lesson each week, it may take some time to adjust. Be patient, you will see transforming results.

How do you get started on your transforming journey? First, talk to some of your contemporaries. Find out what they are using. Is it working? Is it producing desired results? If not, is it the material or the teaching methods being used? Remember, the best material without proper training and methodology of delivery is no better than a bottle of medicine that never comes out of the cabinet. Second, call some Christian education publishers and acquire samples of literature they produce.[7] Also, check with your local Christian Book store for more publishers. Glean the material you receive. Look for the application techniques suggested in this book. Learn from the techniques used by Jesus in the gospels. Which curricula best fits the needs of the learners in your ecclesiastical unit? Next, secure the services of someone well-versed with success in using this type material and training others to use it as well. Contact your denomination office for assistance or contact one of the curriculum publishers for training. Application produces life change. Teach for life change. This is teaching that bears fruit.

Chapter Six

Evidences of Learning

One of the misguided barometers used today in churches and Christian education settings is, "*We are giving them big doses of God's Word every week. If they are not learning, it's their own fault.*" We might be giving them God's Word and big doses of it. The question is, "Can they use what we are giving them?" Are we really giving them anything that is practical in helping them in their walk with God?

I can give you all of the Miracle Grow plant food you can possibly ingest. However, if that is all you have to take into your body, will you remain healthy? Will you grow? After all, it is Miracle Grow. God has created our physical bodies to grow and sustain on a steady diet. If we take the majority of those elements away from our diet, our body will begin to send up warning signals. If we continue to disregard our body, it will begin to shut down, little by little. Our health will deteriorate.

The same is true with our spiritual being. We need a healthy, steady diet (of food digestible for humans, not plant food) to grow and sustain our spiritual being. However, the steady diet many Christians are getting across North America is not the one God has prescribed. An old saying I remember hearing, growing up in Kentucky, regarding preachers or speakers was "All the meat and no potatoes." This meant the speaker had all the substance without any sustenance. Substance is good but it does not produce any evidence of learning. Evidence of learning cannot be found in the lives of most Christian's because they are not receiving the sustenance, which brings about life-change. In many of our churches we are serving up "all the meat and no potatoes."

Some of the big diet phenomenons in the last couple of years are the high protein, low carbohydrate diets. Administered correctly, these diets will work to some extent for most individuals because the body will take in the needed carbohydrates through the allowed food sources, i.e. vegetables and fruits. The body must have a certain portion of sugar (carbohydrates) to sustain proper health. However, in our society today we take in an overabundance of sugars through many food sources. The doctors and creators of these diets understand the need for balanced nutrition. In Chris-

Evidences of Learning

tian education we have seemingly forgotten the need for balanced spiritual nutrition. We must use context for the depiction of God's truths and principles. However, we must also have an earnest portion of application — how do I employ this in my life. Only application will bring forth evidences of learning.

Pastors, teachers, Christian educators, and Christians in general are always looking for "spiritual maturity" in other Christians. Unfortunately, too often we look in the wrong places. As one writer put it, we are using misguided barometers. When we look for spiritually mature Christians we look at what? In most churches, the criteria we use to fill a position is: 1) Attendance, how often are they here? 2) How many jobs in the church do they already have? 3) How long have they been a member of our church? 4) Do they attend Sunday School, Bible study?

While attendance is important and regularity of attendance should be looked at for most positions in the church, is it necessarily a criterion for spiritual maturity? Of course not. Billy Graham has stated that he believes up to fifty percent of the members sitting in our pews every Sunday morning are lost and on their way to Hell. I believe if a person is genuinely saved and maturing in Christ he or she will be in attendance as much as they can be for the fellowship and camaraderie with fellow believers as well as the spiritual inspiration. However, attendance is not an evidence of learning. The level of spirituality or carnality will exhibit evidence of learning or lack of it as they attend the church and its functions.

The number of jobs or positions held in a church definitely is not an evidence of learning. It may be an evidence of need for power or control. It could be a mask for insecurities of salvation or other uncertainties. I have heard men and women brag of the number of positions they hold in the church. One person was boldly telling of being "on three committees and chairman of one, and one of them is the finance committee." He went on to list his other duties at the church as well. Committees may be necessary in your church, but serving on or chairing one is not evidence of learning or spiritual maturity. If the truth were known, most committees do not even serve a ministry purpose nor are they ministry-based or driven. Very little ministry ever takes place in a committee because ministry does not happen in meetings. Most committees spend more than ninety-seven percent of their time in meetings. Serving on committees is not an evidence of learning. The actions of the committee members in and outside the committee meetings will show evidence of learning.

WIDE OPEN BACK DOOR

The length of membership is not an evidence of learning. It is wisdom that uses caution in placing new members into leadership positions in the church. Paul even said new believers should not be pastors for fear of them falling to temptation. I was attending a deacon's meeting several years ago at a church where I was not on staff. One of the elder deacons made the following statement. "I don't believe anyone should be able to serve (in a leadership position) until they have been a member here at least three to five years. Fortunately, for that church, no one else in the room concurred with his statement, at least not verbally.

The problem with his statement is that not everyone joining a church is a new Christian. Perhaps there should be a waiting period to examine their spiritual maturity. However, the back door is standing wide open in many churches today because we do not allow new members to use their God-given talents in our churches as they join. It is my belief that many clergy and most Christians do not realize and fully understand that God has a work (a ministry) for every Christian. He places the right mix of persons at every church at any given time in history to fulfill His purpose for that church at that particular time in history.

Research shows us that if new comers do not have a position of responsibility within three months of joining a church they will leave or disappear. This is where the back door is standing wide open. To help close the back door, many churches are offering classes for new members, assisting the church in assessing the spiritual ability and maturity of new comers to their congregation before placing them in a position for ministry. Allowing members to take on positions of responsibility will certify evidences of learning.

It's All About Change

While regular attendance of Sunday School or Bible study may be considered a needed concern for filling a position in the church, it is not criterion for evidence of learning. If attending Sunday School automatically produced learning and spiritual maturity, our society would have an entirely different make-up today. We have discussed in earlier chapters why learning is not occurring in our churches today. It is obvious that Christian education, be it Sunday School, Bible study, or preaching services has not made a life-changing impact on society in the last thirty to fifty years. To impact society, we must impact the lives of our attendees. While attendance to regular Bible study may show some evidence of learning, the revelation of the evidence of learning comes in how the attendees treat their fellow man. How they live seven days a week, not the impression they make for one or two hours on Sunday morning each week.

One Christian publisher recently ran a campaign focusing on the theme "It's All About Change." Using the following sub-themes they focused on different age groups. "Is his Bible study changing the way he does business?" "Is her Bible study changing the way she views retirement?" Concerning a teenager, "Is his Bible study changing the way he plays the game?" It is all about change. True learning will bring about life-change. The evidences of learning will emerge in our learners' lifestyles in every area of their life outside of the church.

I love the illustration Thom and Joani Schultz use concerning an evidence of learning in their book, *Why Nobody Learns Much of Anything at Church: and How to Fix it.*[8] (Long title but one of the best books

Evidences of Learning

available on teaching). You have been studying the parable of the Good Samaritan. Which of the following best illustrates true learning has occurred?

Student #1 can quote verbatim the story in your preferred translation of the Bible.

Student #2 can tell you the story in his or her own words.

Student #3 can tell you of a time when he/she observed someone being a Good Samaritan.

Student #4 takes a seat at lunch with the student that is all alone and rumored to have AIDS.

You more than likely chose student number four. Yet, which child — or adult — receives the accolades in Sunday School? In most cases it is student number one, isn't it? Are we sending a mixed message to our learners? I think yes. We praise and give stars and ribbons to the student/member who can best quote scripture. Yet, memorization in and of itself is not an evidence of true learning.

Christian educators unknowingly pass on the wrong information. In many cases the student is led to believe, "Memorizing scripture is what pleases God, and I am terrible at memorization, therefore I cannot please God or these people at church." Is it any wonder why so many people leave church at the age of eighteen, many of them never to return again? Innumerable churches are missing one or more decades of ages in their churches. These are a lack of members in their twenties, thirties, forties, and early fifties. It does not take long to assess these are Baby Boomers and those born following the Boomers.

Understanding the Exodus

For years church leaders have blamed the Boomers for causing this exodus from church activity. An entire book could be written on this. In fact some have been written. Let's briefly assess the impact of the church's misguided barometers of evidences of learning might have on this exodus. If it is true that human nature wants and needs acceptance and relationships, why do we lose more than ninety-percent of our teenagers at age eighteen. Acceptance and relationships are encouraged through church activity and the Bible teaches this through God's love. Something that God intended to happen through the local church must be missing. Stronger, or at least more relevant relationships are being built outside the church among teenagers and young adults. Could it be that our misguided understanding of evidences of learning has played a part in this scenario?

When asked why they do not attend Sunday School, many adults report, "Because, I have been there before!" Their report is it is boring. It may be boring because they are not learning anything. Learning is exciting. If true learning is taking place, life-change is occurring, and learning is being evidenced in learners' lives. When this happens, people will return for more and to share their experiences with others of like mind.

At a conference I was leading recently, a gentleman came to me during one of the breaks and said, "I can

Evidences of Learning

relate to what you are saying. We just changed classes at my church and my fourth grade son came home the first week and said he did not want to go back. He did not like his new class." When his father questioned why, he replied his new teacher told the class, "We sit still in this class and don't talk. That's how we learn about God." I thought, "How sad." That teacher just told the children of his class; "In here you will not act your age." I am sure he has good intentions. However, what his listeners heard was, "This class is going to be boring." The evidence of their learning, "I don't want to be here." How much learning will take place in that class? Learning may take place, but not the intended learning. If the learning experience is not interesting and relevant to the students (it must be on their level), the learning you intend to impact upon them will not take place. Unfortunately this very scenario is played out every week in thousands of classrooms in churches of all denominations.

Learning Through Involvement

Are your class attendees going to learn from you giving a thirty-minute lecture on servanthood or from you asking them to help prepare a meal for a family in need? Which one will produce genuine evidence of learning? Involving them of course will produce the evidence. In fact, in this case, the involvement is the learning and the evidence of learning. It is true they could assist in the meal out of a sense of guilt. Even so, they have been involved in a learning experience. A great quote you will read here and elsewhere in this book, "Tell me and I will forget.

Show me and I may remember. Involve me and I will understand." Involvement is practice and brings about evidence of learning.

Will your students learn about helping others by you reading the scriptures of the story of the Good Samaritan and allowing them to color a picture and find hidden words. Or, will they learn by taking part in a food drive

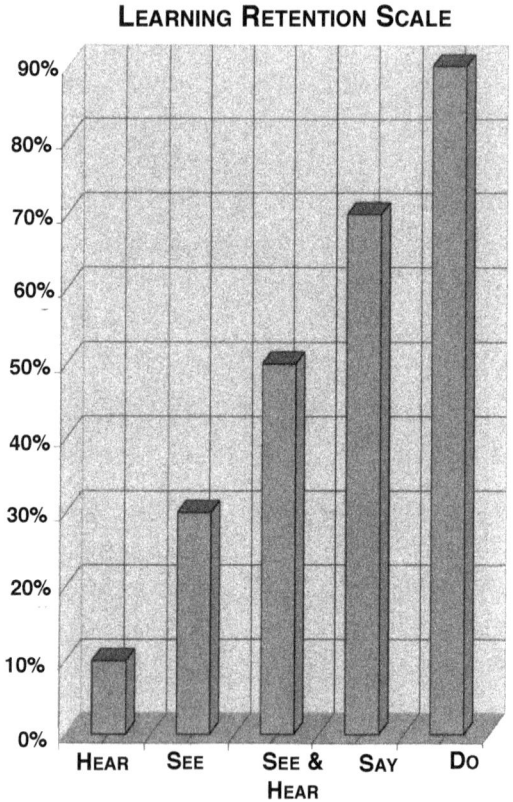

for the local pantry or a hygiene supplies collection for the foreign mission field of a third-world country?

Involve your learners in the learning process. The

learning retention scale shows the higher a person's involvement in the learning process, the greater their level of retention. The learning retention scale shows us that we only remember ten percent of what we hear and thirty percent of what we see.

I remember one of my grade school teachers telling our class that we would only retain about twenty percent of what she would teach us. The other eighty percent would be lost before the year was over. That must have been true, I don't even remember the teacher's name. Our retention increases to some fifty percent if we see and hear the information being related. Research shows that if we say it (the new information) ourselves, retention will increase up to seventy percent. Speaking requires the employment of the Limbic system of the brain. As we formulate sentences in our mind we are processing the information. As we saw in chapter four, the Limbic system not only processes information, it controls memory, emotions and recall. When as learners we are called upon to say the suggested information, our Limbic system is forced into a 'first person' scenario. The possibility of applying long-term memory is greater, yet not guaranteed. Remember rote memorization? It utilizes short-term memory.

When we are called upon to take an active participatory role in the learning experience, our retention increases. As shown in the retention scale, 'doing' can bring results in the ninety percent range. Clearly we see that true long-term learning increases in direct proportion with our personal involvement in the learning encounter. Involve your learners in the learning experience. They will remember! This is life-changing learning.

Which person demonstrates a true evidence of learning about God's love for us, the class member who can quote John 3:16, or the person who spends his summer repairing old fans and delivering them to the elderly living in the ghetto or city projects where there is no air conditioning? People all around the world know of and can quote John 3:16. Yet, how many of our regular, weekly attending, church members really understand what it means? How is John 3:16 evidenced in the way Christians relate to the people they come in contact with each and every day?

Freeze Frame

Stop and meditate on John 3:16. Ask God to share with you the answer to the following questions.

"For God so loved the world that He gave His one and only Son, that whoever will believe on Him will not perish but will have everlasting life!"

You know this with head knowledge. But do you practice it with your heart? How is this love evidenced in your life? Ask God to help you express John 3:16 in how you live everyday. May it be evidenced to the grocery clerks, gas station attendants, bank tellers, and others you meet each day.

True evidence of learning is the outward manifestation of learned principles and truths. Our core values and beliefs are made known through our

Evidences of Learning

actions. Each person has a set of core values and beliefs that are a result of, among other things, our environment, upbringing, relationships, and all prior learning. The way we live and how we treat others is a demonstration of the zenith of our core values and beliefs. A modification in our beliefs (core values) brings about a behavioral change. A behavioral change is an evidence of true learning. It is an outward manifestation of an applied adjustment to our core values.

Watch for evidences of learning in your listeners. How are the truths taught in class being manifested in the lives of your learners? Ask for testimonials. When you see or hear of an evidence of learning confer recognition for it. Make it known publicly. However, use your discretion, some evidences should be left out of the spotlight because they were executed anonymously. Beware of the false evidences of rote memorization, attendance, and others so widely misused today. Observe, watch for, and recognize true evidences of learning. Learning builds upon learning. This is teaching for life-change. This is teaching that bears fruit.

Chapter Seven

Preparation

As a young man, in my early twenties, I would go camping with friends. There were six of us this particular weekend and four had gone to the lake early to set up camp and reserve a spot for the remaining two. Scott and I were going to join them later that evening, after dark. We had not eaten and stopped at the grocery for extra snacks and something for supper. We decided on chicken. So we purchased one and proceeded to the campground. By the way, the one we bought was not precooked as many stores sell today. We were rugged young men and we were ready for some good open-fire-roasted chicken.

It is summer, it is dark and we have not eaten.

Around 11:00 that evening after getting settled in, we built a spit over the fire to roast our chicken. After about forty-five minutes that bird was browning and our growling stomachs were waking the neighboring campers. We were ready to eat but decided to wait a little longer making certain the chicken was cooked. By midnight we could no longer stand it. That browned bird was coming off the spit and we were going to partake in a feast. Our friends who had eaten earlier were delighting in this, by the way. We placed that roasted chicken on a plate and set ourselves down on opposite sides of the table with the chicken between us. We each grabbed a leg and began to twist. As we twisted, the red blood quickly surfaced from the undercooked chicken. That chicken didn't crow or cluck, but our friends were laughing so hard that you could not have heard the chicken if it had.

Why were they laughing? We had set down for a feast, but we had not sufficiently prepared for the feast. (Learning did take place that night!) A few things in life may pass without much preparation, but not the important and teaching is certainly not one of them. If you are going to teach you must surrender to the need for adequate preparation.

OVERLEARNING

Can you imagine the coach of a football team coming to the first practice or any ensuing practice without first preparing? How many football teams take the field on Saturday or Sunday without preparing for the game? Before an NFL team comes out to play on Sun-

Preparation

day each member has devoted a large portion of the week preparing for that particular game.

Don Shula, in his book *Everyone's A Coach*,[9] tells of a routine week for his Miami Dolphins during the playing season. Shula says as quickly as possible following every game played by his team, the coaching staff reviews the film of the game in preparation for the next day (usually Monday) with the players. Monday is to review what happened in the game. Everyone watches the game films as the coaches point out the good and the areas needing improvement. It is also a day to review the physical condition of the players.

Tuesday is the players' day off, but a long working day for the coaches as they prepare for the next opponent. Offensive, defensive, and specialty teams game plans are drawn up for the next game. "A weekly offensive or defensive game plan can run over thirty pages," states Shula. Specialty teams, "can run over twenty pages." Wednesday is devoted to the offensive strategies of the game. It is an all-day session with all coaches and players. That evening when the players leave, the coaches remain and prepare for Thursday. Thursday is the defensive strategy day. Like Wednesday, it is an all day affair for all coaches and players. After the players have all gone for the day, the coaches prepare for Friday. Friday is devoted entirely to the "Red Zone." Or as Coach Shula calls it, the "Green Zone." This is the area of the playing field within twenty yards of the goal line. Football games are won and lost in the "Green Zone." Saturday is put it all together day. Shula refers to it as dress rehearsal day. Sunday is game day. Time to make it happen.

Now retired, Don Shula's football teams were always prepared for the game in front of them. Each player on any of Shula's teams was expected not to think on game day. That may sound strange. However, his teams were so well prepared and fine tuned if a play was not executed correctly or someone was out of place at the end of a play, Shula says nine times out of ten it was because they were thinking about their assignment instead of just doing it. In his book he calls this preparation method—overlearning. He refers to overlearning as knowing the material and assignment so well it becomes second nature to the player. If Christian educators and Christians in general would prepare for every day this way, what changes could be made. What an impact could be made on our society. Are you preparing for your 'game day' (only to teach the lesson) or are you overlearning for the game?

Available Resources

Jesus is part of the Triune God. Yet a reading of the scripture accentuates His preparation. Jesus spent forty days in the wilderness in preparation before embarking on His three-and-a-half years of ministry. In fact He spent thirty years on earth preparing for His ministry. Jesus spent many nights praying—alone with the Father - preparing for the tasks of the days to follow. There were no seminaries, no commentaries for Jesus or His disciples to read. In fact there were very few copies of the written word and they were not read-

Preparation

ily available to the common public. Still, being fully human, Jesus knew the necessity of preparation.

We do not possess the abilities God had in Jesus when He walked on earth. However, He has given us more resources for preparation than any other period in history. What are the resources we have for preparation? We have:

- The Bible
- Commentaries
- Training
- Other Christians
- Internet
- Life's experiences
- The Holy Spirit
- Prewritten curriculum
- Seminaries and Bible Colleges
- Mentors
- Computers
- Libraries
- The world around us
- Prayer

FREEZE FRAME

I have listed fourteen. How many more can you add to the list? Meditate on it. I do not know where the list stops. The boundaries of your mind are the determining factor.

ROUTINE OF PREPARATION

If you teach on a regular scheduled basis it is beneficial to establish a routine of preparation. As in your quiet time each day, I believe you need: 1) a set time of day. 2) A particular place, a room in your home or office free of distractions 3) Divine communication—prayer. 4) Adequate resources—curriculum, Bible, other study helps. 5) A proper attitude, a spiritual frame of mind to allow the Holy Spirit to teach you as you prepare. If you teach weekly on Sunday morning, your preparation for each week could be similar to the one that follows.

Monday, prayerfully read the entire background passage for the lesson. It is good to read the background passage more than once and to read it from different translations. This is also a good time to do a few word studies to help you and your listeners understand the principles and truths. A simple reading of only one translation can cause you to miss an important concept or bias of interpretation needed for your learners to interpret the truth for their lives. I have a pastor friend that reads the background passage no less than six times (sometimes an entire book in the Bible) before he will begin sermon preparation. Read and understand the background passage before moving on in your preparation.

As you prepare from this point in the week always prepare with your individual learners in mind. How will Suzie relate to this scripture or truth? What will be the reaction of Bill and Diane as we relate this truth? How can this principle best be related for those attending to capture the greatest understanding? Preparing with your learners in mind allows the Holy Spirit to guide you in your lesson preparation.

Tuesday, you might begin by reading the lesson from the student book if one is available. Prayerfully read every word in the student book beginning with the title, subtitles, author, scripture references, scriptures, commentaries, activities, footnotes, references, and any other writings that might appear. This will assist you as you study from the leader materials later in the week. I believe it is important that you begin with the student

Preparation

materials, with your students in mind, before moving to the leader materials in order to keep the perspective on your learners and how you will transfer the information and application in a relational manner.

A good question to ask yourself at this point is, "What result(s) should I see in my life and the lives of my learners if I teach this lesson effectively?" Ask for the Lord's guidance in determining the outcome and the avenues to take getting there. "Lord, show me your expected outcome, what changes and new understandings need to occur in our lives as we study and comprehend this scripture?" Once you have determined the desired outcome, begin contemplating the interest level and relevancy of your listeners. Be attuned to the leading of the Holy Spirit. It is vitally important that your conveyance of the lesson be on their level, not only on yours. This is preparing with the learners context in mind and will bring about life-changing learning.

On Wednesday, start with your leader guide. Begin by briefly overviewing the entire lesson. You can do this several ways. Read the focal passages of scripture, scan the different sections and section titles (if available). Next begin by studying the first focal passage. Use your time Thursday and Friday to study and develop your teaching plan for one focal section of scripture each day. It is best to study only one each day allowing the Holy Spirit to guide you in your preparation.

Saturday is the day to pull it all together. Prayerfully assemble the different sections and develop segues from one to the next. Next, you will want to practice your delivery of the lesson. Time yourself as you do a dry run through. Can you deliver the lesson in the time allotted and make it interesting, relational and applicable to all of your listeners? Did you allow time for interaction in the learning process? If not it is time to review what is relevant to your listeners (not to you). What is truly important? If you only had time to deliver one principle, which would it be? Now, what will enable your learners to best understand it and incorporate it in their lives? How can I involve my learners in the learning process to ensure learning? Review for what is truly important. Cut out the rest. You do not need it. In the public classroom and the church what is delivered is fluff. We need to be about the important - the truly important. Jesus was.

As you pull your lesson together on Saturday, pray for each of your learners that might be in attendance the following day asking the Lord to open and prepare their hearts for his message in the lesson. Ask for wisdom and insight in making these principles and truths relevant and applicable in the lives of your learners.

This is only one suggestion for preparing your lesson. You may have one that works as well for you. This may seem to be a stretch for you. This approach generally requires 30 to 45 minutes each day. However, you can spend as much time in preparation as you desire and feel you need to. It is time well spent. Whatever method and routine you choose keep these factors in mind. Always prepare with your learners

Preparation

in mind. Mentally prepare asking questions of how your learners will relate best to the truth being presented. What can be done in the short teaching/learning time to help them integrate God's truths and principles into their lives? Experiment with various teaching approaches and methods. This allows you to prepare relationally. Second, you cannot eat an entire elephant at one sitting. Take the lesson one element, one section at a time. Prepare throughout the week.

Spend the entire week preparing. I have heard teachers state, "I can prepare on Saturday evening and my people don't know the difference." Anyone making a similar statement is telling me they are not trying to teach their class. They are trying to fool their class members. God cannot and will not bless a person with an attitude like that. Preparing through the week is not only good practice it is the growing practice. It allows the Holy Spirit to work through events and circumstances in your life throughout the week to reveal proper delivery and application to you.

After service one Sunday morning, Ron, a middle school Sunday School teacher came by my office. He said, "George, I had to tell you this." He went on to relate this story to me. "Last week I was studying my lesson all week and could not understand how to transfer it to my kids. On Wednesday I just said Lord, 'I can't do this! This lesson isn't making sense to me. I have no idea how to do this on Sunday.'" Ron confessed to me that he had struggled whether to try to teach the scheduled lesson or come up with his own

(Ron knew that is a no-no in my book). He went on to say that Friday evening he was at the office late—a couple of hours late—when one of his fellow employees came by his office and made one statement, a compliment, about his commitment and still being in the office that late on Friday evening. Ron said, "George, I kid you not, at that very second, as soon as he made that statement, everything fell into place. I knew exactly how I was going to deliver the lesson for Sunday. If I had not been preparing all week I would have missed the Holy Spirit's working through that employee and that event to give me my week's lesson. I'm sure glad I didn't wait till Saturday to start (preparing)."

I asked Ron how the lesson went on Sunday morning. He said, with a big grin on his face, "It was one of the best lessons we've had all year." Proper preparation with the Holy Spirit as your guide is not important. It is not crucial. It is critical! There is no other way. Prepare until you are comfortable with the lesson. You can overlearn in your preparation, but do not over prepare to the point that you feel you have to use your dump truck on Sunday morning. Hopefully by now you have parked that dump truck and put a for sale sign on it. (Confused by that statement? Go back and read chapter one).

As you literally prepare and spiritually (prayerfully) prepare, you must also mentally prepare. Prepare with your learners in mind. Know your learners and observe what teaching methods activate their learning styles. Which of Jesus' teaching approaches can you use to produce the greatest learning in your listeners?

Preparation

What will cause them to respond to the principles and truths to bring about behavioral life-change?

I F P A C

A pastor friend of mine, Barry Dollar has developed an acrostic to help him in lesson preparation. It is with his blessing that I share it with you. IFPAC is the acrostic. To many of you this is one more way to package preparation. You may have seen others over the years. I have witnessed teachers turn around in their delivery after a matter of a couple of weeks upon employing this or similar systems in their preparation. There is nothing magical about it. It was not revealed in a vision surrounded by the brightest of lights. It is a good tool to use in developing your lesson for today's generations.

> **I** nterest
> **F** eelings
> **P** rinciples
> **A** pplication
> **C** hallenge

Interest—Create interest through an opening activity. Try to generate interest on an emotional level. Remember, for information to be processed into our long-term memory it must be attached to an emotion. We must realize an emotional benefit for retaining the information. One of the recurring themes throughout this book has been interest. People want to be part of something that is interesting and relevant to them in particular. You may get persons to attend once or even a few times, but if you cannot stimulate interest in your listeners, you will lose them. They will drop out and fall by the wayside. This is one of the greatest downfalls in most churches across North America today. The number one reason most adults give as to why they do not attend Sunday school is, "I've already been there." There is no interest to attend because there was no interest created when they did attend.

Feelings—Feelings in our society today is another word for emotions. Know your learners. Examine their feelings. Ask questions as, "How do you feel after reading and discussing this?" or "What did this exercise bring to mind?" Learn the emotion of a question. Once you have reached them emotionally, you have reached their feelings, you have their interest and you have set the table for learning. True behavioral life-change learning can take place.

Principles—Allow the listeners to discover the principles for themselves. As we have seen through Jesus' teaching and examining learning patterns, self-discovery learning is God's built-in natural learning ability for us. Ask open-ended questions and wait for answers. Give assignments and let them discuss in small groups before bringing their findings to the larger group. Do not answer

Preparation

for them. Rather, guide the discussion in the right direction through their responses. Learning will take place when we allow our listeners to participate in learning. Self-discovery of principles and truths brings about behavioral life-change.

Application—Keep in mind, all of the content and information in the world is of no use unless the learner is able to process and apply it in their life on a daily basis. Create interesting ways to have learners answer the question. What are you going to do about it? How can you apply this in your life this week? Use illustrations, object lessons, questions, practice, and teachable moments to allow learners to discover application for their lives. The more familiar we are with something being presented, the easier it is for us to grasp and understand. Beginning with our attendees' prior learning assists in the learning experience.

Challenge—Each and every lesson delivered should issue a challenge to the learners, be it implied or verbally communicated. What is the desired outcome of the truths and principles of the lesson? The challenge is for each member to implement and integrate God's truths and principles in their daily lives. The challenge must be strong enough to cause the student to be willing to reorganize his or her actions and intentions. That is behavioral life-change. Learners should leave each session with a challenge to commit to something that will draw them nearer to God. *"Draw near unto me and I will draw near unto you."* (James 4:8).

Establish ways to follow-up or remind learners of their commitment to a particular truth or lesson. Perhaps a phone call or note of encouragement for the area of commitment. A visit or lunch with some might be possible. Ask for testimonials at the next class session. Give each attendee a card to write their commitment on. Have them put this in their Bible (or where they will see it every day). Another option is to collect the cards and mail them out in the middle of the week. Be careful not to use any one method of follow-up too often. It will lose its effectiveness. Follow-up breeds accountability.

Utilizing these five distinctives in your lesson preparation, IFPAC, will enhance your teaching and greatly increase the learning capacity of your students. Always prepare with the concern of how to best relate the principles and truths for the greatest understanding by your listeners. Remember to keep the focus on learning, not teaching. Begin with the learners' context. What do they know? What life experiences have they had which will help them in understanding and applying this truth or principle? What methods of teaching can I use to accomplish the desired outcomes? Which of Jesus' teaching/learning approaches could be employed to bring about understanding and behavioral life-change?

Preparation

In most of our classes today there is probably one or less lecture-style learners. Experiment with different teaching approaches — approaches that will bring about learning to the majority of your listeners. Remember each one in attendance has different learning styles. Preparing throughout the week and learning about your people will allow the Holy Spirit to prepare with different approaches. Using methods and approaches that allow your listeners to use their God-given discovery learning abilities will bring about true learning. This is teaching for life change! This is teaching that bears fruit.

Chapter Eight

Interactive Learning

Baheejah lived and taught second grade in Middletown, Ohio when I met her in 1994. She also served on the state science curriculum board. I would listen as Baheejah talked about some of the things that went on in her class. I was intrigued at what the young students were enabled to do in the name of learning. I thought, "I might have gotten more out of science if my classes were more like hers." I went to visit her second grade class one morning and found something I did not expect. I expected desks lined up in straight rows, all facing the front of the room with the teacher's desk and a chalk board that covered the front wall. Instead, what I found were desks arranged in groups of four, two side by side facing two more, side by side. These 'pods' as they were called were scattered around the room. Students were facing different directions. My thoughts were, "How could a teacher stand in the front of the room and teach (lecture) like this?"

I found out she did not stand in one place. The teacher walked from pod to pod encouraging and assisting each student as the lesson of the hour unfolded. That morning I also found a classroom of students well-behaved but not silent. They were orderly, yet, not stiff and staunch. As I entered the room, I heard children engaged in conversation and laughter. They were loud yet productive. This teacher had learned to harness the energy and creativity of young children to generate learning. Without raising her voice, Baheejah spoke to the class in a normal voice and introduced me as her friend and gave my name. In one accord the students all said, "Good morning, Mr. Yates."

The teacher's desk and blackboard? I am sure they were there, no classroom would be complete without them, would it? If she had a desk and blackboard in the room, they were so obscure that they blended into the teaching/learning environment. These items did not have the ever-looming presence as when I went to school. Like this classroom in Middletown, Ohio, some teachers and schools systems are moving to a more conducive learning environment.

A few years ago my wife and I hosted a foreign exchange student. In getting to know Ruth, our exchange student, she related how the schools were different in New Zealand, her home country, from

Interactive Learning

ours in the United States. One seemingly major difference was in New Zealand, Ruth had experienced as much learning outside the classroom as inside. Much of the learning in her home country was done in 'labs' which really were not labs as we know them. Their learning was done in the fields, mountains, streams, woods, and public venues. As Ruth recalled it, more time was spent outside rather than in the classroom for science, biology, and physics classes. The natural environment was often used for the setting of math classes as well. Imagine using real life settings as our classrooms. I recall reading of another teacher who taught that way—Jesus.

Interactive learning is important for all areas of learning and all ages. However, there may be different levels of interactive learning applied for various age groups. Earlier chapters in this book illustrated Jesus' approach to teaching. Jesus used different means of interactive learning with His learners. Jesus knew the importance of interactive learning. Let's look at the six approaches discussed earlier and see their relevance to interactive learning.

CONNECTING PRIOR LEARNING WITH THE NEW

First, *Discovery learning*—Does it require interaction? Yes it does! The student must participate in the learning experience. Discovery learning requires the learner to call upon prior learning and exploration of the stated or implied principle of the current learning situation. Discovery learning begins with the context of the learner's prior knowledge and the probing intellect to search out significance of the present learning circumstances.

Second, *Object lessons*—Interaction? Yes! Object lessons impel interactive learning through visuals. These visuals call upon prior learning through the stimulation of brain waves and thought processes of a prior knowledge of the object being presented. When an object is placed in front of a viewer's eyes, the brain automatically recalls any prior knowledge of that object. The new information being related is now attached to the prior learning. The interaction between the student and the object lesson is one of the most penetrating methods of learning available.

Third, *Illustrations and parables*—These create interactive learning by causing the learner to paint a mental picture of the story being related as it is told. For this to happen, the cognitive ability to call upon prior learning must be present. For example, if I relate to you a story about a gunfight at the O.K. Corral, your mind paints a picture of a western scene in the 19th century. If I speak to you of a personal trip of mine to McDonald's, you have certain images come to mind. Just mentioning this has caused your mind to paint a picture from your memory bank including those famous golden arches. Jesus used many illustrations and parables because He knew the cause and effect of connecting prior learning with the prevailing experience.

Fourth, *Teachable moments*—Jesus used teachable moments knowing when His learners were engaged in an activity, they were ready to learn. Teachable moments seize advantage of what is impacting the lives of the learners at the very instant to communicate a learning experience for the learners.

> **FREEZE FRAME**
>
> *Your learners are on an outing together and one member is stung by a bee. A teachable moment has arisen for various topics. What topics might you utilize the situation for?*

In this situation, a teachable moment has actualized for, the vulnerability of every person, the need to care for hurting individuals, first aid and other topics you may have realized. Teachable moments create interactive learning by using the present situation to give birth to learning.

Fifth, *Practice*—Practice is putting into action the principles of the learning experience. Practice solicits interaction as the learner must become involved in the learning process. Practice is the modeling or role-playing in the class setting. It is also the day to day activity and our attempt to live Christ-like. Jesus allowed His learners to exercise or perform what they had observed from his teachings. Practice comes from simulating life's experiences in the classroom and through living our lives daily.

Sixth, *Questions*—Utilizing proper lines of questions prompts interactive learning by activating the higher-order thought processes. To comprehend a question, each learner must employ the cognitive elements of the brain, stimulating the personal concept of conviction of the principle being challenged or queried. Proper use of questions will challenge a person's belief system. A person's belief system is formulated by all former acquired knowledge. When a challenge is issued, the cognitive system begins a course of action bringing former information to the foreground and causing the brain to minutely examine the challenge and new information with the former. It is by dissecting and comparing the two that allows the brain to reformulate the belief system. Questions definitely compel interactive learning.

Interaction occurs when we stimulate the brain and the thought processes of our learners into action requiring a response from each learner. A verbal response is not always imperative at the point of interaction (in the classroom setting). The point is not to achieve a verbal response. It is to bring about behavioral life-change. However, if higher-order thinking is not activated and existing beliefs are not challenged, learning cannot take place.

Interactive learning can be deployed differently for various age groups. I have often wondered though, why we stop using certain types of interactive learning with adults. I recently was asked to lead a youth group in a Wednesday night Bible study. After praying about a topic and a delivery method, I decided to devote my entire time to a game of Concentration. I set up my game board with numbered squares (1-12). After dividing the room

Interactive Learning

into three groups (teams) and explaining the game to all participants, I pulled up a stool and accepted the role of game show host.

Under ten of the numbers were five words and five definitions. There were also two blanks that had to be matched to complete the puzzle. The teams had to match the word to the proper definition. The five words were—1) confession, 2) adoration, 3) thanksgiving, 4) intercession, 5) petition. The puzzle behind the clues read "Five Parts of a Prayer."

To some this may seem a little unorthodox. However, most of those youth will remember more of the parts of a prayer today and two years from now than they will most sermons or Bible studies given in a lecture style. Why? Because the learning experience was totally interactive for them. Did they learn more about how to pray? For our debrief session after the "game," we used scripture and group discussion techniques to examine how each part of the prayer is important to each of the learners present that evening and all Christian teenagers.

I saved the game board for about a month thinking I might challenge our adult teachers to use something similar with their classes. Instead, I challenged them with this line of questioning. Why do we not use something like this with adults? I admitted I did not normally use a game show take-off in an adult teaching setting. However, I have used them on numerous occasions with teens. Then I asked this question. What is one of the most talked about TV shows among adults today? It is "Who Wants To Be a Millionaire." What about Jeopardy, and Wheel of Fortune? Do your class members watch those shows? Some adults watch certain game shows with a passion. In fact some adults are more religious about and dedicated to their favorite game shows than they are church and their work for the Lord. Game shows call upon the interaction processes of the mind. Could you create interest with your learners fashioning a take-off of a game show to illustrate a point or principle in your next lesson?

DEBRIEF

Let me throw out a word of caution here. Any learning activity used in class (game show, small group or individual discussion, exercise, drama, or other activity) must be followed with a debriefing session to ensure every participant relates the exercise with the learning expectancy. A debriefing session is a time to bring all participants together to delineate what happened in the exercise to cause the participants to arrive at the confirmed outcome, how it relates to the principle of the lesson being studied, and how the outcome will affect the lives of the participants. The debriefing session is the mortar that bonds or cements the understanding of the principles behind the activity to the long-term memory. Without the debriefing, the memory is of an isolated activity with no bearing on learning.

FELLOWSHIP

As the name implies, 'interactive' learning compels learners to respond to the activity going on in the classroom. This happens only when the teacher moves beyond the lecture/monologue style of delivery. Students are not only compelled to interact with the teacher. They are led to interact with each other. This is healthy and motivating in the learning atmosphere for several reasons. Some we have discussed in earlier chapters. Others we have not. One important factor is the innate desire God has placed within each of us to have *koinonia* — fellowship with others. Interactive learning institutes fellowship between learners, which helps foster and build relationships. As relationships develop and mature, people are inclined to share more freely and become more involved. Each week or each session, learners become more comfortable in their relationships with other classmates and the learning atmosphere increases within the group. As the learning atmosphere increases, consequently the learning is enhanced as well.

ELEVATE LEARNING POTENTIAL

Interactive learning creates interest on behalf of the listener. Remember IFPAC. It all begins with interest. Capture their interest and you'll captivate their desire for learning. Utilizing interactive learning elevates the learning potential of individuals by engaging higher-order thinking. The stirring of the higher-order thought processes gives birth to new learning by using as its foundation prior learning. Our cognitive development operates under this principle. Learning is based upon learning. When someone is explaining a new recipe to you, they do not have to define or draw a skillet or sauce pan for you. You already know what those utensils are (prior learning). You only need to know the ingredients, how to prepare them, and what temperature and length of time to cook the intended menu item.

Interactive learning creates interest, helps build relationships, calls on prior knowledge and learning, and engages higher-order thinking. Once enacted, the higher-order thought processes allow the Holy Spirit to produce life-change learning. Interactive learning engages the listener in the learning process, thus it becomes a learning process. Using interaction in the teaching/learning process translates into life-change. Teach for life-change! This is teaching that bears fruit.

Chapter Nine

Time Thieves of Christian Education

In 1994, I authored a study titled "Biblically Based Time Management." In this study, one session is titled "Time Thieves." There are many things that rob us of precious time in our daily lives. Sitting in traffic, interruptions, waiting in lines while shopping, meetings, and unexpected down time due to accidents and equipment failure are just a few. There are also distinct time thieves in group Bible study and teaching time as well. I want to take a look at some of these in this chapter. Some I believe should never be used in Christian education because they do not aid in the learning process. In actuality, many of these deter and negate learning, as well as send a confusing message to the learner.

The publishers of Christian education curriculum provide some of our time thieves while we create others ourselves. The ones our publishers create are the 'busyness' or the 'time filler' activities they supply. These may include word scrambles, jumbles, encoded messages, crossword puzzles, dot-to-dot, fill-in-the-blanks, seek and find puzzles (both word and pictorial) and other non-creative activities. Most of these are placed in our curriculum without the realization that they are not actual teaching material. Others, however, are placed for time fillers in order to try to offer the Christian educator or teacher, ample material to 'fill' the hour.

Litmus Test

Any activity presented in the teaching/learning session should contribute to the learning process by promoting higher-order thinking at the proper age level. Christian educators can use this 'litmus' test for activities to present during the learning session: 1) Is this in any way going to contribute to, or reinforce the desired outcome of learning for the session? 2) If so, how? 3) Does the answer to question number two promote higher-order thinking that could bring about behavioral life-change? If the answer to one and three are a definite yes, then keep the activity in the lesson. If, however, there is any doubt or question in the validity to the possibility of learning, discard the activity.

One other test is, can you debrief the activity to tie it to the learning objective for the session? Every activity in the session should be followed by a debriefing session, giving a clear depiction of how the activity reinforces the truth or principles studied and possible activation of said principles in the learners lives. Never should an activity be used in class without immediately being followed by a debriefing session.

Here are a few samples of what we can find in some of our literature. In this first one, the students are to interpret the code to find the biblical truth.

The encoded statement above says, "God is love." However, you first must decipher the code, then translate the statement before you can understand what God is. What are we telling our students with this type of curriculum?

RLSMUBENAC

Scrambled words appear in children's curriculum quite often. What learning in the Christian education setting can possibly come from unscrambling words? These are time fillers. The answer to the scrambled word—unscramble.

Crossword and Seek and Find puzzles are also favorites of publishers. Here are two that I used years ago as a Youth Pastor. I will admit I did not use these as time fillers in Sunday School or other Bible study. I used these at lock-ins or fun nights. However, looking back I don't know how many teenagers considered this fun. They did the exercise to humor me I guess. And for the free pizza afterwards, of course.

Across

1. The first King of Israel
11. Moses brother
12. Saw the first rainbow
25. ___ of Galilee

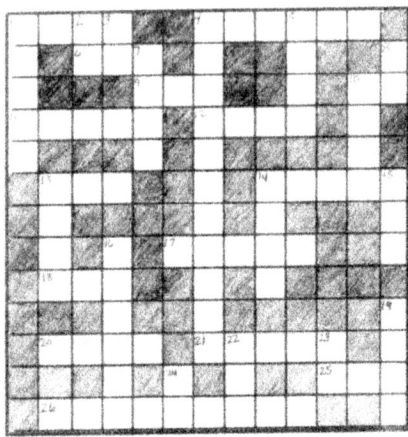

Find The Books of The Bible

```
E O N O M E L I H P B J O B S O X A D
L Z E P H A N I A H E N O M U Z E P R
E H E C C L E S I A S T E S D J B O I
V I C K N G I I S G R A E T O N E P N
I K C O I K S S O G V Y S R X O M S E
T R A P S E E E M A L J E R E M I A H
I S A I A H L N G I O P A S M O C L E
C A J M K S C E T E R S Q U E L H M M
U B I L O R I G L O J O N A H D A S I
S E M A J E N B A D A M N E G S A X A
H A I D A B O R M A L A C H I F P E H
S E S T H M R O E N R E N Q K O I T L
B T C O M U H A N I O E U A S G N I K
R R E C E N C I T E M Z H M P N M L O
E A U H S O J B A L A R I T A O L E W
V I K U S U T I T U N A L H S S O L E
O F K P R O M N I K S S T C A E S O H
R M A R K I T H O E D U J Z A G P A T
P O B O C Y M O N O R E T U E D S L T
O R A A G E N J S I X D U X R U D G A
J E H A I R A H C E Z G E D O J E B M
```

Time Thieves of Christian Education

Some of these activities in and of themselves are not always necessarily bad. Men and women work crossword puzzles everyday. Some do it to sharpen their intellect. Some do it for fun. You can find Seek and Find puzzles in daily newspapers around the country. However, if we are using them as teaching tools we are deceiving ourselves and confusing our learners. We are sending out a shrouded message that God is mysterious, confusing, and hidden. My God is a bold, upfront, and open God.

In my office, I have a copy of a workbook for new Christians which is distributed by a certain ministry for churches of multiple denominations. The workbook contains five lessons and is intended to be used in a class setting or in a one-on-one mentoring situation. However, many times this book is given to new Christians and they are left to complete the work by themselves. There is no paragraphed reading in the booklet. It is line after line of fill-in-the-blank statements with scripture references for each line. The following is a simulation of what you might find in this booklet.

> Because we all have sinned, we are destined to _____. (Romans 6:23)
> God does not want _____ to _____. (2 Peter 3:9)
> Your ____ has separated you from _____. (Is. 59:2)
> These things have I _____ unto you... that ye may know that ye have _____ _____. (1 John 5:13)

Jesus said to him, "I am the way, the _____, and the _____: no man cometh unto the _____ but by me. (John 14:6)
Behold I stand at the _____ and _____ ... (Rev.3:20)

The first lesson in this book is five pages containing sixty-four fill-in-the-blanks with scripture references bouncing back and forth in the Old and New Testaments.

FREEZE FRAME

Remembering this book is for new Christians, what are some of the obscured or hidden messages being sent to the new believer with this type of curriculum?

There is a hidden agenda in this book and other materials written for adults as well as other age groups. Some of the obscured messages being received from this particular new Christian piece is: 1) "I do not understand what all of this means. Is God a God of misunderstandings?" or 2) "This church stuff is confusing. If God is this confusing already, I'll never make it." 3) "How am I supposed to know where to find all of these? I don't even know what all these abbreviations stand for or what these names mean." 4) "They could at least put these in order. I don't know where I'm at or where I'm going. Is that what God is all about?" 5) "This is too much like work. I'm not going to waste my time on this. I've got important things to do."

It is important to remember we are dealing with new Christians. These are persons who may never have looked inside a Bible before. To a new believer this is all foreign. It looks confusing, difficult, and unimportant not only for new Christians for veteran Christians as well. Not to mention it does look a lot like unnecessary schoolwork of days gone by. We can be our own worst enemy when it comes to discipling other Christians and new converts.

As I travel around leading and attending conferences, I have noticed a couple of other Bible study time thieves appear in many classrooms as well; too much fellowship time, overextended prayer request time, and late comers. Teachers around the country seem to have these in common.

KOINONIA

I am a firm believer in fellowship time for Bible study members. At our church we have named our Sunday School as other churches have, Bible Fellowship. It is where we come together as a peer group to study the Bible and to enjoy *koinonia* - fellowship. True *koinonia* does not wait for Sunday morning at 9:30. It is a 24/7 adventure. It does begin and revolve around our Sunday morning group time. But it does not end there. It is carried throughout the week.

I encourage teachers to begin class with a fellowship time. People are not only looking for a friendly church today, they are looking for friends. God has designed us with an innate desire to have fellowship with others of like-mindedness. It does not matter how large or small your church is, relationships cannot be fostered or nurtured in the worship center. This is where small groups, Bible study groups such as Sunday School classes can and should play a significant role. People need a place where they can meet people and build relationships and the church has a responsibility to supply that avenue. A book could be written on the many experiences that have been shared with me or I have witnessed from classes that have truly grasped the understanding of what God intended *koinonia* to be. Yet, all of those experiences come from less than three percent of classes in churches today. Sadly, many churches do not have even one class with a minimal understanding or practice of this true *koinonia*.

The dilemma of too much fellowship time arises when teachers cannot bring the fellowship portion of the class to a close to begin the lesson teaching time. While fellowship time is good and an intricate part of a growing (spiritually and numerically) class, it must not cut into teaching time. Good quality fellowship time is needed in our society today. However, we must learn to control it in order to move into the teaching time. One way to do this is with "Total Time Teaching." You can use total time teaching by having a starter activity for the learners as they come into the room. Some weeks you may have chairs set up in small groups to encourage group discussions with something related to the lesson for the day.

It is my opinion not to use a scripture related activity as the pre-class opening activity. Rather, use a current event or a personal encounter activity. Some examples might be - As members arrive ask them to discuss in small groups—1) How current trouble in the Middle East affects their family and your church. 2) How has God provided for you in the past? How does that affect the way you live today? 3) How do you feel when a neighbor or family member continues to come to you to borrow tools, yet never brings them back in as good condition as when borrowed?

Other alternatives to opening activities are to prepare a board or tear sheet on a wall with a statement or question similar to those mentioned above. Ask each person to write a comment about the suggestion on the tear sheet as they enter the room. You might use something as; "How has God provided for you when you least expected it?" or list the most memorable Christmas of your childhood. When you are ready to start the teaching time, draw everyone's attention to the pre-class activity and ask for responses. This way your attendees will enjoy fellowship time and be prepared for your initiation of the lesson as well.

Freeze Frame

What pre-class activities could you use if your lesson was concerning the following. (List at least two examples for each)

The Ten Commandments

Jesus' anger in the Temple

Paul and Silas singing at midnight

Remember this exercise as you prepare your lesson. There are innumerable activities to use for pre-class warm-ups. This will prepare your learners for the lesson and for true learning by stimulating the thought processes even before you begin to teach.

PRAYER

Prayer requests are another essential part of the Bible study class. There are, however, a couple of pitfalls teachers and classes find themselves in. May I suggest two considerations to assist in avoiding those pitfalls? First of all, determine the reason you meet together. If it is for Bible study then the bulk of the time should be devoted to Bible study. Keeping this on the forefront of class members' minds will help, especially when you need to bring the prayer request time to a close. Once you have determined priority of the class meeting you can establish prayer request guidelines if necessary. Suggestions I have made in the past include passing a prayer request sheet around the room during the fellowship time. The class secretary or prayer leader can make photocopies and hand them out at the end of the class. This allows you to focus on the other class priorities without neglecting anyone's request.

I know of one class that has as their guideline, "We only allow prayer requests for salvation of family and friends. There is a Wednesday night prayer meeting and a prayer ministry for all other requests." That may sound a little brute at first. What they have done is executed a way to be about the important. What is priority one on Sunday morning? Bible study. Ask any of the ladies in that class their opinion, including the one's that have been saved through the prayer and evangelism efforts of the class members. There are 167 additional hours in the week for prayer and prayer requests. Corporate Bible study time is precious and should be guarded. Sunday morning, is all about Bible study to change lives.

One other time thief notable of mention is teacher overkill. This is a time thief being overused in Christian education settings across the country and around the world. This time thief has been examined at length in previous chapters under different designations. This occurs when a teacher teaches under the belief that he or she must cover all of the material and unload (dump) all the information they have gleaned in several hours of study into a thirty minute teaching session. Your learners cannot learn this way—at least not what we hope for them to learn.

At a recent meeting of teachers of adult Sunday School classes, one teacher stated he was having trouble covering all the scripture in the lesson and using examples and activities of application in the short allotted teaching time. As he explained, he related that he tries to bring his learners up to date by giving them the history behind the scriptures being studied. Then, he of course tries to explain the scriptures for the day and attempts to make application for those scriptures. One of his peers affirmed him this way: "I used to do the same thing. Until I learned (understood) that we don't teach the Bible. We teach the people in our class."

My explanation of that statement is the Bible is God's Word. We cannot teach the Bible or God anything. We are called to teach our learners how to live the way we are instructed by God's Word. Another teacher in the meeting admitted, "I used to study eight to ten hours a week preparing my lesson. Now, I spend about three hours, because I am learning I don't need the history (in class on Sunday morning). They do not learn from all the history. I am trying to give them application." Learning *is* taking place in his classroom on Sunday morning.

The teachers concurred that people attending the class want something besides a history lesson when they come to Bible Fellowship. They want to know, "What does this mean to me? How can I draw closer to God with what you are telling me?" The first teacher asserted, "So if I'm hearing you right, I should spend less time on preparing my lesson and use that other time in a personal Bible study, or contacting my (class) members."

Is that what the other teachers were saying? Absolutely! They were not saying, don't waste time studying. They were saying get rid of the 'fat.' If it is not necessary to get the principles and truths out to your learners, why spend valuable time researching it and delivering it. Content is important. But content does not change lives. Application changes lives. Teach to change lives. This is teaching that bears fruit.

Conclusion

Christian education has strayed from its original intent and goals throughout much of North America. We teach the way we were taught. While it is true we process more information through our brain today than any other time period in history, Christian educators supply 'information overload' and it cannot be processed by those sitting in our classes. We must move beyond the lecture—monologue mindset. Our teaching methods must be interesting and relative to those in attendance. We must break the mold of "teaching the way we were taught" and learn to teach using the methods of "The Master Teacher," Jesus.

This will require training. It is a process. It will not happen overnight. It is a process for the Christian educator and the learners as well. My prayer is that this book is the catalyst to move you to begin that process and the stimulus to push forward on your journey to teach for life-change.

First you will need to determine what you intend to teach. Are you going to teach the Bible? No, the

Bible is God's Word. It cannot be improved upon. Are you going to teach the curriculum? No, the curriculum is nothing but mere paper and ink. It cannot learn. It has been formulated and put into writing to assist you in leading your learners. As Christian educators our call is to lead others in the understanding of the principles and truths within the Bible. Helping them to use these principles and truths to reformulate their beliefs will cause behavioral life-change, an increase in their spiritual maturity and allow them to continually draw nearer to God.

Once we know what (who) we are teaching, we need to know our learners. Draw near to them as Philip was drawn to the chariot of the Ethiopian eunuch (Acts 8). Observe your learners in and out of the class. How do they act and react? What are some of their life experiences? What can you learn about your learners that will help you in your lesson preparation? Always prepare your lesson with your learners in mind.

Take advantage of every training opportunity that you can avail yourself to. How can anyone teach who is not willing to be taught? It matters not what vocation you are in or what you do in life, there is always amended and updated training. Teaching for God is so much more significant than any occupation. We must continually seek to strengthen and grow in our abilities. God gives us our full measure when He gifts us. Yet He expects us to grow and develop in those gifts throughout our lives. Ascertain various teaching methods and

Conclusion

approaches. Then practice the different ones. Utilize diverse methods in class each week or each session. You have different learning styles in your class. Your students need varying methods to accommodate those learning styles. Teach as Jesus taught. Use the teaching methods He used.

Learn to use interactive learning in your class. If you expect learning to take place, you must provide the opportunity for learning. If what you do in class does not stir the thought processes by generating higher-order thinking, learning cannot transpire. Learning builds upon learning. Interactive learning engenders learners to call upon prior learning to bring about life-change.

Dare to move beyond who you are and who you think you are. Strive to be all God has called you to be. Every time you sit down to prepare for your class call upon God to use the Holy Spirit to enlighten you for His deliverance of the scriptures into the lives of your learners. The Holy Spirit is the only true Christian education teacher. Only He can bring about true life-changing learning.

> *"I am the vine, you are the branches; he who abides in Me, and I in him, he bears much fruit; for apart from Me you can do nothing."*
> John 15:5

A teacher has not taught until someone has learned something. The true success of any teacher is measured only by the successful behavioral life-change of his/her learners. Teach for spiritual transformation. Teach for life-change. May God bless the seeds of your teaching that they may bear fruit for many years.

Endnotes

[1] Webster's II New Riverside University Dictionary, 1984

[2] Ibid.

[3] Ibid.

[4] Thom and Joani Schultz, *Why Nobody Learns Much of Anything At Church: And How To Fix It,* Group 1993, p. 34.

[5] Rick Yount, *The Teaching Ministry Of the Church,* Broadman & Holman, 1995, p. 196.

[6] Bruce Wilkinson, *Seven Laws of the Learner,*

[7] David C. Cook, Group Publishing, LifeWay Christian Resources, Standard Publishing.

[8] Thom & Joani Schultz, *Why Nobody learns Much of Anything At Church: And How to Fix It,* Group, 1993, p. 21.

[9] Don Shula, Ken Blanchard, "Everyone's A Coach," Harper 1995, p. 82.

To learn about more resources from George Yates, visit SonC.A.R.E. Ministries at http://soncare.net or check out your favorite on-line retailer.

www.ingramcontent.com/pod-product-compliance
Lightning Source LLC
LaVergne TN
LVHW051603070426
835507LV00021B/2747